The Bible On
Asceticism

The Bible

on

Asceticism

by H. WENNINK

Translated by F. VANDER HEIJDEN

ST. NORBERT ABBEY PRESS
De Pere, Wisconsin
U. S. A.
1966

Biblical quotations are from the Revised Standard Version of the Bible, copyrighted 1946 and 1952 by the Division of Christian Education, National Council of Churches, and used by permission.

2UP
W4P7E

Nihil obstat:

Samuel D. Jadin, O. Praem.
Censor deputatus

Imprimatur: 163£06

†Stanislaus V. Bona, D.D.
Bishop of Green Bay
April 27, 1966

Originally published as
De Bijbel over Ascese
Roermond and Maaseik, J. J. Romen & Zonen, 1964

Library of Congress catalogue card number 66 - 16988

Printed in the United States of America
ST. NORBERT ABBEY PRESS
De Pere, Wisconsin

CONTENTS

INTRODUCTION

Few concepts are more closely connected with Christianity than is asceticism. It connotes an attempt to express Christian belief as perfectly as possible in a special way of life. If we speak of it from a different viewpoint — as is done in other religions, or even in sports — we usually feel that in a sense it still derives from Christianity. It may therefore be surprising to note that the Bible does not speak explicitly about asceticism. It seldom mentions either the word or any of its derivatives. When we do find it, we discover that it is not used in a specialized technical sense. We meet it only twice, once as a verb meaning "striving" (to keep a clean conscience, Acts 24:16), and once with reference to the Sabbath: 2 Macc. 15:4). We can not speak of a univocal concept of "asceticism" in the Bible.[1]

The Greek term, from which our modern word was derived by way of Latin, has, when used technically, an ancient Christian origin. In a wide sense it means a life of true piety in any situation, including the worldly; in a stricter sense it means following the ideal of Christian perfection in a special way of life. So an ascetic might have been either a fervent Christian in the world, or one who lived in celibacy.

The word may have acquired its formalized meaning in Christianity because of its development in pre-Christian Greek paganism. The meaning of the Greek verbal form evolved from "to fashion something artificially" (Homer), "to make something fit by artificial fashioning," to "to apply oneself to something," "to exercise oneself." Thus the Greek word took on the general meaning of **a methodical endeavor,** zeal to reach some ideal or human perfection in some area — bodily (athletes and soldiers), philosophically (wisdom), ethically (virtue) or religiously (contemplation of God).

Thus it is somewhat understandable that Catholic theology came to describe asceticism as a special methodical endeavor (inspired by grace) of a Christian in his ascent to Christian perfection. From this definition it is evident that it can also exist in other religions and philosophies of life. In these too one may find a certain methodical human endeavor to strive toward perfection. But further definition of this concept will depend on the way different religions and differing philosophies think about the nature of human perfection and the way this ideal is to be obtained.

We can give a somewhat more specific description of asceticism by distinguishing three types: moral, cultual and mystical. Moral asceticism means a certain self-discipline which tries to obtain an exact equilibrium between the different powers in man, thus fostering a harmonious development of the human person Cultual asceticism embraces certain practices (usually connected with worship) by which man prepares himself to participate in the sacred, divine sphere. Mystical asceticism means bringing oneself by methodical exercises to immediate experience of the divine.[2]

This distinction does not mean that the three types of asceticism are found in isolation or clearly and distinctly separated. Nor does it mean that these adequately comprise all phenomena which could be considered ascetic. But it may be of some use in describing the nature and development of asceticism as found in Biblical revelation. We will see that none of these three types is necessarily and positively incompatible with the Biblical concept. We will also find that Scriptural asceticism, as revelation progresses, develops from the more cultual to the more mystical. Moral asceticism, which need not have a religious character, will not necessarily determine the proper nature of Biblical asceticism.

One important question should be answered: How can we speak about "The Bible on Asceticism," if neither the word in its technical sense nor a sufficiently clear idea of what it is can be found in the Bible?

A superficial look at the table of contents of this treatise will explain how we have solved this difficulty: we have examined the stance taken by the Bible in regard to earthly values and realities. It will be made sufficiently evident that this subject is of real importance in the Bible, and that it is also of great importance for asceticism itself. We can provisorily explain this. It often appears difficult to keep to a happy mean in asceticism. Deviations depend largely on the standpoint one takes regarding things of this world. Different and often extreme opinions about this have developed in the course of history, frequently basing themselves on isolated Bible texts.

Therefore it is important to make a survey of the entire Scriptural position in this regard, thus providing ourselves with a norm for sound asceticism and enabling us to distinguish the genuine from the inauthentic in certain ascetic practices. Christian asceticism has a long history in which we see various developments. This is why, if it is to remain pure, it must always return to the Bible as to its source. It may not return only to certain classic texts. It must return to the realm of the entire Biblical world of faith in which these texts — often because of their seeming contradictions — have their function and wherein they can be correctly understood.

By using this wide interpretation we believe that we will be able to give a real answer to modern man who asks what the Bible has to say about asceticism.

POSITIVE ATTITUDE
TOWARD THE WORLD

Our introduction attempts to define asceticism according to the mind of the Church today. We made no allusions to practices which are often considered ascetic, such as self-castigation, privations, difficult exercises in prayer, uncomfortable postures, etc. These arose as a reaction against exaggerated hedonism and worldliness. Even today, they portray a particular viewpoint of man and the world which gives a distorted concept of asceticism.

In the course of history the Church often condemned heresies which considered matter to be the principle of all evil and saw an irreducible opposition between matter and spirit, body and soul. This dualistic pessimism was the error of the gnostics and the Manicheans of the first centuries of Christianity, and of the Cathari of the middle ages. It was revived by Descartes, a philosopher of the early seventeenth century.

Modern times have their own trends which distort the image of Christian asceticism. Seventeenth century rationalism and the marvelous progress of modern science today caused violent clashes between faith and human reason. The old familiar world-image of antiquity and of the Bible, in which man hitherto had felt safe and which had its influence on the preachings of Christianity, was shaken to its very depths by the findings of modern science. To safeguard her deposit of faith the Church withdrew and went on the defensive. Since she neglected the definitive findings of modern times for too long, she maneuvered herself more and more into an isolated position. She lost contact with modern science and alienated herself from the modern world. The protestant Bible scholar Rudolf Bultmann was influential in making the Christian message again acceptable to our modern times. He proposed an **entmythologisierung** (demythologizing) intended to strip the testimony of Biblical faith of its primitive antiquated formulas and to adapt it to our modern way of thinking. His philosophical viewpoint in his exegesis of the Bible however reverted to the age-old dualism with a modern touch. His distinction between the objective and the existential structure of time supposes an irreducible opposition between matter on the one hand and spirit and God on the other.[3] According to his concept Christian perfection would consist in being free of the encumbrances of matter, and asceticism would practically be identical with renunciation of the world.

The irresistible progress of modern science with its undeniable service to human welfare, has given man an ever increasing appreciation of the material reality of his existence. Especially since World War

II Catholic theology has begun to focus attention on earthly values. Regarding Christian asceticism as conceived during the past centuries, some have asked if it still has any reason for existence. Representatives of comparative religious sciences believe that it is a residue of an arachronistic philosophy of life. Psychologists think it manifests a lack of courage to accept human responsibility in this world. Should modern, educated and spiritually integrated man reject asceticism?

1. Pre-gnosticism of the apostolic period

Our question, in reverse, was already discussed in the second half of the first century. The Bible then took a stand which would appeal to a modern man's heart. It is remarkable that the progressive tendency of those days showed a great preference for an asceticism of world renunciation and self-castigation.

About 60 A.D., in the eastern Mediterranean area, a religious movement preached a possibility of man's redemption through "gnosis" (knowledge). The climate of the Roman empire at that time was ready for this new way of thinking. Several religious systems adopted this philosophy and its ideas penetrated into Christianity. In Paul's letter to the Christians of Colossae (during his first Roman captivity, 61-63) and in his letters (between 64 and 67) to Timothy and Titus, bishops of Ephesus and Crete, it is evident that he had been confronted with this gnosis in several churches. He writes somewhat vaguely about it perhaps because it was not yet a clearly defined doctrine; it was rather a manner of thinking which threatened to infect the young Church. He speaks about "teachers of the law" (1 Tim. 1:7; cf. 6:20 and Col. 2:16), "vain discussion" (1 Tim. 1:6; cf. 6:5; 4:20; 2 Tim. 2:14, 16, 23; Tit. 1:10, 11 and Col. 2:4, 8, 21, 23), about "myths and genealogies" (1 Tim. 1:4; 2 Tim. 4:4; Tit. 1:14), "who forbid marriage and enjoin abstinence from foods which God created" (1 Tim. 4:3-4; cf. Col. 2:16, 21, 22 and 2:18, 23). These texts indicate that he refers to Jews or Jewish Christians who were propagating this nefarious way of life. He clearly shows his abhorrence. They "make their way into households, . . . oppose the truth, men of corrupt mind and counterfeit faith" (2 Tim. 3:6, 8); "and their talk will eat its way like gangrene" (ibid. 2:17).

In his letter to the Christians of Colossae Paul enunciates a sublime theology when he expressly points out that the only Mediator and Redeemer is Christ, in whom "the whole fullness of deity dwells bodily" (Col. 2:9). In his pastoral letters he is less constructive. He here commits his disciple-bishops to defensive tactics. He says: "Guard the truth that has been entrusted to you; follow the pattern of the sound words which you have heard from me, in the faith and love" (Tim. 1:13-14; cf. 1 Tim. 6:20; 1:10; 6:3; 2 Tim. 4:3; Tit. 1:9, 13; 2:1, 2, 8; 2 Tim. 2:2).

At the end of the first century, the aged apostle John had to cope with the same difficulties in Asia Minor. Despite his age he shows remarkable adapt-ability when he refrains from simply rejecting the gnosis. He uses its practical elements to build a "modern" Christian message. This explains the unusual form of his writings, his gospel and his letters. Especially characteristic of his gospel is the irreconcilable opposition between God and "this world"; he elaborates this by the antitheses of light and darkness, life and death, truth and lie. He also often stresses "knowing" God (it is remarkable that he never uses the noun "knowledge"). Dualism, as manifested in his gospel (but in an entirely different sense), was exactly the basis of gnostic thought.

The real battle between gnosticism and Christianity however was fought in the second century. Therefore we only know the true nature of this movement, long since grown into heresy, from post-apostolic writings. But we can to some extent describe the spiritual position established by Paul and John.

Our material world, gnosticism says, is so impregnated by corruption and evil that an exalted God could not possibly be concerned with it. God and the world are as opposed as are light and darkness. Man, a spark from the realm of light, has been thrown into the darkness of the material world. Knowledge (gnosis) makes him realize his miserable condition and leads him back to his original communion with the divine light. Only initiation gives this knowledge to man; it is given through a revelation from beyond this world. A realm of higher and lower superterrestrial beings maintains contact between the deity and gnostic man. Christ is one of these intermediate beings; but his revelation cannot be a divine call for this corrupt world and its history, except in appearance only (docetism).

John's resistance to this heresy is vehement: "By this you know the Spirit of God: every spirit which confesses that Jesus Christ has come in the flesh is of God, and every spirit which does not confess Jesus is not of God. This is the spirit of antichrist, of which you heard that it was coming, and now it is in the world already" (1 Jn. 4:2 ff.); "For many deceivers have gone out into the world, men who will not acknowledge the coming of Jesus Christ in the flesh; such a one is the deceiver and the antichrist" (2 Jn. 7). If Jesus Christ was not truly the incarnated Son of God (cf. also Jn. 1:14) he could not possibly suffer and consequently has not died nor risen. The historicity of God's entrance into this world would be nothing but an illusion, as is the existence of Jesus Christ himself (cf. 1 Jn. 4:3). Gnosticism also denies that we can really speak about a redemption from sin. We can only be liberated from matter. It therefore denies any obligation to moral conduct. Hence John says emphatically: "And by this we may be sure that we know him, if we keep his commandments. He who says I know him but disobeys his commandments is a liar, and the truth is not in him; but whoever keeps his word, in him truly love for God is perfected. By this we may be sure that we are in him: he who says he abides in him ought to walk in the same way in which he walked. Beloved, I am writing you no new com-

mandments, but an old commandment which you
had from the beginning; the old commandment is the
word which you have heard. Yet I am writing you
a new commandment, which is true in him and in
you, because the darkness is passing away and the
true light is already shining. He who says he is in
the light and hates his brother is in the darkness
still. He who loves his brother abides in the light,
and in him there is no cause for stumbling. But he
who hates his brother is in the darkness and walks
in the darkness, and does not know where he is
going, because the darkness has blinded his eyes" (1
Jn. 2:3-11).

Mystical union with God, in gnosticism, ultimately
is not God-given. It is brought about and extorted
by an ascetic technique of renouncing the world.
"Knowledge" for the gnostic is based on a mythological self-projection; redemption therefore is not by
grace of a God who freely reveals himself. It is
self-redemption. To gnostic ears Jesus' words in his
high-priestly prayer could only be senseless prattle:
"Father, the hour has come; glorify thy Son that thy
Son may glorify thee, since thou hast given him
power over all flesh, to give eternal life to all whom
thou hast given him. And this is eternal life, that
they know thee the only true God, and Jesus Christ
whom thou hast sent. I glorified thee on earth,
having accomplished the work which thou hast given
me to do; and now, Father, glorify thou me in thy
own presence with the glory which I had with thee
before the world was made" (Jn. 17:1-5).

2. God and human history

From this controversy between ancient Christianity
and gnosticism it is evident that their concepts of
asceticism were different because of their differing
views on the relationship between God and the
material world. It is true that this gnostic philosophy
of life shows that it wrestled with the problem of
evil in the world. This appeals to many modern
people. It also appealed to the Bible authors, as we
shall see in our third chapter. But the Sacred Books
do not lapse into the extreme pessimism of gnosticism, which could not accept God as the creator
and ruler of the material world. Scriptural testimony
is positive on this point: God created heaven and
earth and saw that they were very good (Gen. 1).
Innumerable texts glorify God because of his creative
work: "The Lord by wisdom founded the earth, by
understanding he established the heavens" (Prov.
3:19; cf. 8:22-31). "O Lord, how manifold are thy
works! In wisdom hast thou made them all; the
earth is full of thy creatures" (Ps. 104:24). It
extends repeated invitations to praise God, because
"the Lord is a great God, and a great King above
all gods. In his hand are the depths of the earth;
the heights of the mountains are his also. The sea
is his, for he made it; for his hands formed the dry
land" (Ps. 95:3-5; cf. Ps. 119:73, 90 ff.); praise him,
for "by the word of the Lord the heavens were made,
and all their host by the breath of his mouth . . ."
(Ps. 33:6); "The earth is the Lord's and the fullness
thereof, the world and those who dwell therein; for
he has founded it upon the seas, and established

it upon the rivers" (Ps. 24:1-2; cf. Ps. 89:12 ff.; "Woe to the nations that rise up against my people! The Lord almighty will take vengeance on them in the day of judgment; fire and worms he will give to their flesh; they shall walk in pain forever" (Jud. 16:17).

Other psalms are invitations to sing God's praises because of his creation: 8; 19:1-17; 136:4-9; 148; cf. also the doxologies in Amos 4:13; 5:8 ff.; 9:5 ff. In the "Book of Consolation" the anonymous author ceaselessly appeals to the fact that the entire world, even including darkness and evil (Is. 45:7), was created by Yahweh (40:26; 43:1, 7, 15; 45:7, 12, 18; 54:5 etc.). The New Testament preserved the dogma of creation as an enduring element of faith: "All things were made through him (the Word of God), and without him was not anything made" (Jn. 1:3 ff.; cf. 1 Cor. 8:6; Eph. 3:9 etc.). Paul makes effective use of this dogma in his fight against liars ". . . who forbid marriage and enjoin abstinence from food which God created to be received with thanksgiving by those who believe and know the truth. For everything created by God is good, and nothing is to be rejected if it is received with thanksgiving; for then it is consecrated by the word of God and prayer" (1 Tim. 4:3-5).

To see the true nature of Biblical asceticism we must make a deeper study of the real relationship between God and the world. This is also relevant for our own time. Man easily falls into extremes. In countering the exaggerated pessimism of a dualistic philosophy of life as found in ancient gnosticism, he is currently inclined to adopt an equally exaggerated optimism. The progress of science and technology, especially as seen in an evolutionary milieu, sometimes induces modern man to take an attitude of autonomous self-realization.

A Christian too has an optimistic view of the material world. But his optimism is entirely inspired by Scriptural faith in the historical reality of God's saving activity during his earthly existence. The exact meaning of this will become evident from another confrontation: Biblical faith and hellenistic gnosticism.

Ancient peoples, especially the Greeks, were impressed by the wonderful rhythm of the universe. Everything appears to act according to a pattern of ascent and descent, of appearing and disappearing, of life and death. This is manifested in the alternation of day and night, in the waning and waxing of the moon, in the regular succession of the seasons, in the phenomena of life and death in all domains — vegetal, animal and human — in the rising but ever again declining of the generations. This constant rhythm appoints everything to its place and creates a world of perfect harmony. Grecian man, full of admiration for this universal order, called the universe **cosmos,** which means "order." From this cosmic harmony Plato (5-4th century B.C.) deduced the existence of a God, who in his kindness orders all things for the good of man. The constant rhythm of the course of the world, without the slightest variation, gave the impression that time in our material world is circular and consequently has no beginning and no end; as a result, there really is no past and no future. This was not sufficient motivation for Plato to express belief in a benign divine providence.

The later stoics also spoke about providence, but what they meant by this was the hard unchangeable law of nature which mercilessly rules all existing things: Fate. Endless repetition of the same constant rhythm holds man in its grip. Man has no defense against evil which has its own place in this universal order. The gods are preoccupied only with themselves; they remain indifferent to the lot of man. In a letter to his friend Lucilius, Seneca (Ep. LXX ad Lucilium) suggests the following line of conduct against suffering: "The most beautiful rule of the eternal law is that it allows us only one entrance into life, but many exits. Why should I wait for a terrible illness or a cruel man if it lies in my power to evade all terrors? The only reason for not complaining about life is that we are not bound to it. Life therefore has been ordered very well: nobody has to be unhappy, unless through his own fault. If you are satisfied, enjoy life. If you are dissatisfied, then you can return to where you came from." Seneca himself died, as a true stoic should, by suicide. Every stoic who was not yet tired of life tried to acquire a proud indifference to all that fate had in store for him; and he always had Seneca's fine means of escape at hand.

Although stoicism may have produced individuals who compel admiration for their strength and personality, its ethics lacks all real religious foundation because of the human pride on which it is based. So-called stoic asceticism is really nothing but the practice of a certain self-discipline and escapism, with the possibility of suicide for those who tire of life.

For the gnostic the visible world is not the result of a watchful providence. The cycle of time makes our material world, infected as it is by corruption, a hopeless vale of tears. World time is the counterpart of eternity; the gnostic antitheses of matter and spirit, darkness and light, evil and good are after all only variations on the contrast between time and eternity. Hence gnostic asceticism, in its renunciation of the world, also refuses to accept time.

It is this latter refusal which makes gnosticism a heresy. Biblical optimism as regards the material world is based on the belief that God as a person freely and intensely preoccuplies himself with the concrete lot of man in this world. Actual divine intervention in this worldly human existence determines the structure of time and, in doing so, it also determines the lot of humanity. In Paul's speech in the Areopagus in Athens the Bible helps us surmise how Christianity really differs from Greek thought. According to Luke's report, Paul says: "God . . . having determined allotted periods and the boundaries of their habitation . . ." (Acts 17:26). The Athenian public here heard a thesis familiar to their own philosophy of life: the regular succession of the seasons are the work of a providence. But this phrase — as well as the whole speech of Paul — can be explained in two ways — a Greek way and a Biblical-religious way. Luke's description of the speech shows that Paul tried to minimize the contrast between the Scriptural message and the hellenistic world-view. The Greeks understood "times" in a quantitative sense, namely, as exactly and objectively measured distances, not differentiated in themselves. Their "habitations" are spatially divided by boundaries. The "times" therefore are considered especially as to their duration; the Greeks measured them by the regular movement of the celestial bodies. Semitic thought, as is evident from the sacred writings, looks at time in a much more concrete way: it qualifies time. As for sun and moon, Biblical man does not so much pay attention to the duration of their movement as to their radiation of light (cf. Gen. 1:14 ff.; Ps. 136:7). "Seasons" are described by what is spontaneously experienced in them: there is "the time of the rains" (cf. Lk. 26:4; Deut. 11:14; 28:12 etc.), and the time in which the wadies dry up (Job 6:17). Everything, every action, every event has its own time: "For everything there is a season, and a time for every matter under heaven: a time to be born, and a time to die; a time to plant, and a time to pluck up what is planted; a time to kill, and a time to heal: a time to break down, and a time to build up; a time to weep, and a time to laugh; a time to mourn, and a time to dance; a time to cast away stones, and a time to gather

stones together; a time to embrace, and a time to re-
frain from embracing; a time to seek, and a time
to lose; a time to keep, and a time to cast away; a
time to rend, and a time to sew; a time to keep
silence, and a time to speak; a time to love, and a
time to hate; a time for war, and a time for peace"
(Eccles. 3:1-8).

Thus the semite, in his religious considerations,
was inclined to define time according to the concrete
importance it had for him. His faith taught him that
God also has his times — his time of benevolence
(Is. 49:8; Ps. 69:14; 1 Cor. 6:2) and his time of
wrath (Jer. 18:23; Ps. 21:10). This is exactly what
characterizes time in the Bible: it is determined,
in the last resort, by God's salutary actions. The
meaninglessness of endlessly succeeding moments is
done away with, because each moment means an
invitation to a community in love with God; the
totality of progressing time includes new stages in
the ascent toward perfect union with him. Biblical
time is not cyclical but linear. It is history, because
it is the reflection of the love drama between the
Creator of the world and the humanity he created
— a drama with all the comforts and trials of
matrimony. This is the real significance of God's
salvation plan: having been hidden from eternity in
him, it has, after an age-long gradual revelation, only
been revealed and realized to the full in the incar-
nation of the eternal Word in Jesus Christ. In this
God-man the decisive "yes" is spoken between the
Father and the human race he created; the true

Covenant, a communion of love, has been entered upon for all eternity. This was the message Paul wished to convey to the Athenians: "The times of ignorance God (salvation being accomplished in Jesus Christ) overlooked (Acts 17:30). "Having determined allotted periods" (Acts 17:26), or in other words, having impressed his special seal on the lot of all peoples of the earth, God has made the times significant by making them instruments of salvation.

From what we have said we may now conclude what constitutes the special nature of Scriptural salvation, namely, the reality of historical salvation in our concrete human existence — the fact that God is present in our material world to lead us, by way of a covenant of historical community of life, to imperishable union with him in eternal happiness. Gnosticism denied this presence of God in the world, and saw no other way to beatific union with him except through an asceticism which liberated man from the body and from all that was material. Gnostic dualism therefore fundamentally justifies all forms of corporal castigation, renunciation of material goods and turning away from this world.

The real error of this gnostic philosophy of life is its doctrine that matter and its temporalities are essentially correlative with evil and liability to disintegration. For this reason, it ascribes the creation of the material world and its changeableness to rebellious beings, powers of darkness. Man, who lives in this temporal, and consequently corruptible,

world looks for salvation in a systematic asceticism
which will allow escape from his corporeality.

In the Bible however existence in time is not
essentially correlative with corruptibility and liability
to disintegration. Through God's grace it leads to
life and happiness for anyone of good will. By his
body man is subjected to the cosmic rhythm of time,
but he transcends this by being a spirit. Biblical
faith in the living reality of the God of the Covenant
in our earthly existence makes man conscious of the
fact that he stands in a time whose rhythm is distinguished from and exalted above cosmic time. The
revealing God who calls man gives him the consciousness of being a free person, whose development
to fullness is the result of a religious surrender, the
invitation to an ever more intimate communion of
love with him. Man is essentially a historical being
and the Bible knows this because God made time an
instrument of man's future salvation. Biblical faith
in God as the creator of the material world is based
on this. Consciousness of this determines the Biblical
view of asceticism. Accordingly the sacred authors
do not see asceticism as **essentially** connected with
escape from the world, as does gnosticism. A positive
attitude toward the world is necessary. We will give
concrete illustrations of this point from revelation.

3. The Biblical positive attitude toward the world, as faith received from grace

In the history of human thought we note a tension
between the spiritual and the material. We may

say that modern times try to correct a too spiritualized bias of the past. Thus it happens that today
we may feel ourselves less akin to the spiritualizing
Greeks than to the material minded people of the
East. Evanescence of all creaturely things was no
reason to question the meaning of human existence:
it belonged to the very nature of all corporeal things.
In the old Israel it was said as a matter of course,
though not without regret, that man when dying
"went the way of all the earth" (Jos. 23:14). The
psalms ask God to let man live, because neither man
nor God profits by his death; after his passing he can
no longer praise God (cf. Ps. 30:10; 88:12; 115:17).
From such a viewpoint only a postive attitude toward
the world can give meaning to life on earth.

This attitude toward life came naturally to the
chosen people, even before they were addressed by
the God of revelation; but they were able to make
this their own ideal only by way of a gradual revelation. Let us now see how the positive attitude of
the Bible was a logical consequence of faith in the
God of revelation as a historical reality.

The Sacred Writings testify that God, in and
through time, realizes a plan of salvation for the
world; also, that the people of Israel had a very
special place in the concrete realization of this plan.
We find this religious faith expressed in the story
of Abraham's vocation: "Now the Lord said to
Abraham: Go from your country and your kindred
and your father's house to the land that I will show
you. And I will make of you a great nation, and I

will bless you, and make your name great, so that you
will be a blessing. I will bless those who bless you,
and him who curses you I will curse; and in you all
the families of the earth shall be blessed" (Gen.
12:1-3).

In the development of this religious consciousness
we can distinguish the following stages:

(a) Israel discovered God's historical contact with
the world on its own **national level.** It was aware
that it had been chosen by God in preference to all
other peoples. Among these other peoples God allowed himself to be discovered through the created
world. But he made himself known to Israel by
personal intervention in their existence. The so-called
Deuteronomic tradition expressed this belief in the
following words: "The sun, and the moon and the
stars, all the host of heaven, . . . things which the
Lord your God has allotted to all the people under
the whole heaven. But the Lord has taken you . . .
to be a people of his own possession" (Deut. 4:19-20).

Israel is the chosen people and Yahweh is its God.
The Bible shows what this meant in the vision of
Moses' vocation (Ex. 3:7-10, 13-15). When he receives
from "the God of the fathers" the task of liberating
the chosen people from the slavery of Egypt, he
asks the name of Israel's God. He receives the
answer: "I AM WHO I AM" (Ex. 3:13-15). In a
popular etymology of the name "Yahweh," the author
here gives us a description of the nature of Israel's
God. With this "I am" the Israelite is not simply

expressing his belief in the mere existence of his God. For him there is no doubt about this. Nor is this a philosophical statement about God as "existence itself." The Israelite, in his concrete way of thinking, by this name means that his God is a God who is actively present, intervening, helping. By his faith he knows that his God is really concerned with the lot of his people: in times of distress by his saving intervention, in case of disobedience by his punishing hand. We should also note that the sacred writer, in explaining the name of Yahweh, does not give any further explanation of this "being": "I am who I am" is quoted absolutely, without qualification. Israel's God claims this name for himself as exclusively his own. He does not share it with other gods, his "being" is not described more precisely as a special kind of being. His being knows no limits, it comprehends all, without any regard to place or time or person or situation. In short, he is divine actuality in the full sense of the word. For Israel this meant that their national God is absolutely transcendent, but at the same time and exactly because of this, he is also really immanent. He is the exalted supreme being, infinitely mysterious and ineffable; yet he is always directly and intensely preoccupied with the existence and the history of everything in this world. It is obvious that from the beginning Israel was not explicitly aware of just how comprehensive and incomprehensible this national God of theirs really was. But revelation of the name "Yahweh" in a seminal way continued the possibility that Israel could later call its national God the God of the whole world.

"The God of the fathers" disclosed his true identity
to Moses when he made known his plans to liberate
the sons of Israel from the oppression of Egypt.
Yahweh was also the God who liberated them from
slavery. The dramatic and epic way this liberation
from Egypt is described in the Bible[4] shows its deep
rooted conviction of Yahweh's eminent power: it is
he alone who saves.

Israel belongs to Yahweh and Yahweh belongs
to Israel. Liberation and covenant are always closely
joined in the Bible: the covenant is the guarantee of
final liberation: "You have seen what I did to the
Egyptians, and how I bore you on eagles' wings and
brought you to myself. Now therefore, if you will
obey my voice and keep my covenant, you shall be
my own possession among all peoples; for all the
earth is mine, and you shall be to me a kingdom of
priests and a holy nation" (Ex. 3:4-6).

Through the covenant Israel is taken into a living
communion with Yahweh. The ritual of entering
upon the covenant near Mount Sinai as described in
Ex. 24:3-8 is a concrete expression of this religious
conviction. Moses reads Yahweh's conditions for the
covenant to the people and they agree to them.
After this the altar (which represents Yahweh) and
the people are sprinkled with the same blood (the
seat of life, cf. Lev. 17:14). Both parties are now
partners in one commonly shared destiny: the lot of
the people is also the lot of Yahweh. His covenant
with his people had the characteristics of a communion of love. For this reason the prophets speak

of it as a marriage. In the history of the people of Israel their covenant and marriage were always considered a guarantee of ultimate salvation.

(b) This covenanted relationship was subjected to a great crisis by a fault of the chosen people. This was really to be expected. Yahweh's saving presence initially manifested itself on a material level: liberation from the slavery of Egypt, proving that Yahweh was stronger than Egypt's military power; protection during the desert journey against hunger, thirst and hostile tribes; the conquest of Canaan, a land that flowed with milk and honey; liberation from conquerors during the period of the judges. All this was sufficient reason to arouse feelings of nationalism and materialism in Israel. Moreover, since this was an old eastern people, it was easily inclined to make its relationship to God a magic one, to take its destiny into its own hands by negotiating, as it were, with its national God. All this is incompatible with the nature of a community of love, as the covenant of Yahweh with his people should be. The prophets often reproached Israel for its misbehavior. Great national calamities, such as the abduction of the northern kingdom into the Assyrian captivity (722 B.C.) and of the southern kingdom into the Babylonian captivity (586 B.C.) could have been spiritual transfusion for their faith. The period of Israel's prophets is the apogee of Yahwist doctrine.

Though Yahweh's saving activity first expressed itself in a material way, from the very beginning the great good resulting from his saving intervention was himself and the peoples' communion with him. All other effects derived their value from this alone. Thus we read how Moses and the children of Israel, overawed by Yahweh's display of power in their passing through the Red Sea, sang this song in his honor: "I will sing to the Lord, for he has triumphed gloriously; the horse and his rider he has thrown into the sea. The Lord is my strength and my song, and he has become my salvation . . ." (Ex. 15:1 ff.). After the horrible sin of the people near Mount Sinai Moses succeeded in reconciling them again to the Lord who says: "My presence will go with you and I will give you rest. And he (Moses) said to him: If thy presence will not go with me, do not carry us up from here. For how shall it be known that I have found favor in thy sight, I and thy people? Is it not in thy going with us, so that we are distinct, I and thy people, from all other people that are upon the face of the earth?" (Ex. 33:14-16). Yet only the prophets announced explicitly that **Yahweh alone** was the real source of salvation in all its forms; more than this, he was also **real salvation** itself. The prophets announce their approaching doom to the people of Damascus and Samaria: "For you have forgotten the God of your salvation, and have not remembered the Rock of your refuge" (Is. 17:10). In Micah a badly beaten Samaria expresses its confidence in future redress: "But as for me, I will look to the Lord, I will wait for the God of my salvation; my God will hear me" (7:7; cf. Deut. 32:15; Ps. 68:20 etc.). Jeremiah, the "prophet of calamities," in his exhortation to conversion, teaches the people of Judah where to look for real salvation and to say: "Behold, we come to thee, for thou art the Lord our God. Truly the hills are a delusion, the orgies on the mountains. Truly in the Lord our God is the salvation of Israel" (3:23; 14:8 ff.).

Prophetic preaching, founded on an authentic religious faith in Yahweh directs Israel's attention to a more spiritual and more universal view of salvation after physical calamities like the Babylonian captivity (586-539) had humbled Israel. These taught them that Yahweh's active presence reached further than Israel and its national territory. They became aware that in the future "all flesh" would see Yahweh's salvation (Is. 45:22; 49:6; 51:5). Thus the idea of the covenant was purified of narrow nationalism and raised from a collective to an individual level: "Behold, the days are coming, says the Lord, when I will make a new covenant with the house of Israel and the house of Judah, not like the covenant which I made with their fathers when I took them by the hand to bring them out of the land of Egypt, my covenant which they broke, though I was their husband, says the Lord. But this is the covenant which I will make with the house of Israel after those days, says the Lord: I will put my law within them, and I will write it upon their hearts; and I will be their God, and they shall be my people. And no longer shall each man teach his neighbor and each his brother, saying: Know the Lord. For they shall all know me, from the least

of them to the greatest, says the Lord; for I will
forgive their iniquity, and I will remember their
sins no more" (Jer. 31:31-34; cf. Ezek. 16:59-63;
also 36:25-29).

(c) The vision of the prophets always penetrates
more deeply into the mystery of Yahweh's nature
and sees **redemption** as a real **creation**. In the very
beginning of its national history Israel had expressed
its belief and conviction that the people gives
thanks for its existence to the living God alone who
had raised (from the barren and aged Sarah) a people
numerous as the stars in the sky and the grains of
sand on the seashore (cf. Gen. 17). Belief that they
had been brought into existence by a creating redeeming God really comes to the fore only at the
height of the period of the prophets. Only then do
they really become conscious of the all-embracing
aspect of Yahweh's being (cf. above). Israel in its
totality is solely the effect of Yahweh's creative
salvation: "Do you thus requite the Lord, you foolish
and senseless people? Is not he your father, who
created you, who made you and established you?"
(Deut. 32:6). The conviction that Yahweh is their
creating God who saved their nation sustained Israel
during the hardships of the Babylonian exile: "But
now, thus says the Lord, he who created thee, O
Jacob, he who formed you, O Israel. Fear not, for
I have redeemed you; I have called you by name,
you are mine" (Is. 43:1; cf. 43:7, 15). With such a
consciousness, it was easy to see Yahweh as the
creator of the world, as the one who had called

"heaven and earth" into existence, entirely (Gen. 1).
It is not surprising that this conviction was expressed
so explicitly during the Babylonian exile in the Book
of Consolation (Is. 40-55): "Lift up your eyes on
high and see: who created these? He who brings
out their host by number, calling them all by name;
by the greatness of his might, and because he is
strong in power, not one is missing" (40:26; cf. 40:22).
"I am the Lord, and there is no other. I form light
and create darkness, I make weal and create woe,
I am the Lord who do all these things" (Is. 45:6 ff.;
cf. 45:12, 18). "For your Maker is your husband,
the Lord of hosts is his name; and the Holy One of
Israel is your Redeemer, the God of the whole earth
he is called" (54:5). "Thus says the Lord, your
Redeemer, who formed you from the womb: I am
the Lord, who made all things, who stretched out
the heavens alone, who spread out the earth — Who
was with me?" (44:24).

Yahweh's power is without limit. He is the creator
of the universe; he is also the ruler of the destinies of
peoples. He summons Cyrus the king of the Persians
for the salvation of Israel (Is. 41:1-5, 25; 44:28; 45:1-6,
13; 46:11), and he makes other peoples a ransom for
the redemption of his people (Is. 43:3-4). His saving
will encompasses all peoples (cf. Is. 45:14-16, 20-25
etc.). His sovereign power rules over death and life.
The apocalypse of Isaiah (24-27) predicts that he will
"destroy on this mountain the covering that is cast
over all peoples, the veil that is spread over all
nations" (Is. 25:7 ff.). At the end of time "many of

those who sleep in the dust of the earth shall awake,
some to everlasting life, and some to shame and
everlasting contempt. And those who are wise shall
shine like the brightness of the firmament; and
those who turn many to righteousness, like the stars
for ever and ever" (Dan. 12:2 ff.; cf. 2 Macc. 7:9,
11, 14, 23; 14:46). For Israel Yahweh prepared a
future "everlasting salvation" (Is. 45:17; 51:6, 8), and
in the so-called Third Isaiah (56-65) he announces
"For behold, I create new heavens and a new earth;
and the former things shall not be remembered or
come into mind. But be glad and rejoice for ever
in that which I create" (65:17; 66:22). Yahweh is the
absolute sovereign who rules all history: its beginning
is from him (cf. Gen. 1), as is its end (cf. Gen. 49:1;
Num. 24:14; Is. 2:2; Hos. 3:5; Ezek. 38:16; Mic. 4:1).
"I, the Lord, the first, and with the last, I am he the
Lord says" (Is. 41:4; 44:6; 48:12). Finally climaxing
all human history there will be, according to Biblical
faith, the "day of Yahweh," the day on which for
the last time he will enter into the history of mankind and sit in judgment over the eternal destiny of
all peoples (Joel 4:4; Zech. 14).

(d) The New Covenant is the complete fulfillment of the expectation of the Old. Here we find
mentioned the "last times" and similar expressions
(cf. Acts 2:15 ff.; 1 Cor. 10:11; 1 Pet. 4:7; 1 Jn.
2:18); the "Day of the Lord" (cf. Acts 2:20; 1 Cor.
1:8; 5:5; 2 Cor. 1:14; 1 Thess. 5:2; 2 Thess. 2:2;
2 Pet. 3:12; Rev. 16:14). Characteristic of this New
Covenant, the power of Yahweh is now handed over

to the risen Lord (cf. Mt. 28:18; Jn. 3:35; 5:21 etc.). Whatever is said in the Old Testament about Yahweh (cf. above) is now said about Christ: He is the Lord of life and death (cf. Jn. 5:21), without whom nothing was made (Jn. 1:3; Col. 1:15-20; Heb. 1:1-3), the universal Redeemer (cf. Acts 4:12; Jn. 4:42), Lord of all human history; he is "the Alpha and the Omega" (the Beginning and the End) (Rev. 1:8; 21:6; 22:13). That all creation still looks forward to his return does not do away with the fact that "the Day of Yahweh" has already dawned. According to John, Christ himself says: "Now is the judgment of the world" (Jn. 12:31; cf. 3:18 ff.). It therefore is a characteristic feature of the spirituality of early Christians that their whole life is based on the conviction that the "last days," "the day of the Lord," has already begun, although final fulfillment is still to come. In other words, Christ is exercising final judgment over the world now. This is a reality within our world, not outside it. Final judgment does not mean the end of a material world, but indeed its total re-creation. Is it not characteristic of the faith-view of the Bible that, just as it pictures the original paradise in a truly "earthly" way, so also on its last pages (Rev. 21:9; 22:5) it depicts the future eternal paradise in earthly colors — heaven descending upon earth (cf. Rev. 21:10)?

CONCLUSION

From a general description of asceticism as a methodical endeavor to strive after Christian perfection we have seen that the Bible does not understand this as an escape from the world, self-castigation or renunciation. On the contrary, from the very beginning Biblical man adopted a positive attitude toward the world. The chosen people accepted this and made it entirely its own, founding it on the Yahwist faith it had acquired. The New Covenant also preaches an appreciation for earthly values; Paul explicitly defends these against rising gnostic errors.

We have seen that the Scriptural concept of asceticism was ultimately based on the religious conviction that human existence in this world is controlled by the historical presence of the God of salvation. Its belief in God as the creator of the world and its appreciation of material things is also based on this same conviction. It is important that we understand this point of view. From it follows the fact that asceticism cannot simply be a question of periodic actions or assumed attitudes; it really implies a continuously exercised behavior pattern. The existence of the saving God affects me at every moment of my life and imposes upon me a constant obligation, an uninterrupted effort toward perfect union with the God of my salvation. Asceticism therefore is a daily affair, and a very Christian affair (not only for members of religious orders or for saints). Here is one reality which is the same for all concerned. In our daily life we can distinguish ascetic actions or attitudes, certain heights in the everyday rhythm of life, which emphasize and confirm the general pattern.

From a correct understanding of the special nature of Scriptural asceticism we should be able to explain certain practices which at first seem to be a contradiction to the concept we have described. For example, in the course of the centuries penitential practices of some saints (Benedict Labre, the curé d'Ars) were sometimes considered "inhuman." If the nature of asceticism is determined by the historical reality of the redeeming God then its final norm must be found in the sovereign will of this redeeming God. As we have said above, it is he, according to the Bible, who sealed the time of our human existence in a special way. The moments of time are his invitation for us to enter into constantly growing communion of love with him. The norms we use must be deduced from a common sense view of this earthly life. The sovereign will of the historically present saving God is the last word. What in the eyes of the world may seem sheer madness may be highest wisdom before God. This is what Paul said (cf. 1 Cor. 18:3-4).

It is evident that the thesis we are defending in this our first chapter has relativity. We shall clarify this further.

RENUNCIATION OF
THE WORLD

At the end of the last chapter we concluded that certain ascetic practices of some saints could be explained by the historical character of the God of salvation. But what could induce this saving God, without a doubt the creating God, to make relative this appreciation of the material world, in these cases and in others where Biblical revelation speaks about the "end time" (cf. chapter 1). Why should he ever put an end to this world? Why should he, by imposing severe ascetic practices, sometimes order man to reject earthly values?

We shall now try to give an answer to this question.

In the Bible we find some actions which indicate a rejection of earthly reality. We must be careful however, if we wish to classify these as asceticism, to arrange them all under a common denominator.

One of the first things which strikes us in the Old Testament is a system of rules for purity. Some of them concern certain sexual phenomena (cf. Ex. 19:15; Lev. 15:18-24; 1 Sam. 21:5), death (cf. Lev. 21:1 ff., 11; Num. 5:2; 19:21-22; Hag. 2:13), certain ill-

nesses (such as leprosy: Lev. 13-14), certain animals
(cf. Lev. 11:1-47; Deut. 14:3-20), food (cf. Lev. 19:11;
17 etc.) and war cf. 1 Sam. 21:6; 2 Sam. 21:6; 11:11).
In all these rules the Israelite saw a concrete description of conditions which made a worshipful communion with the exalted saving God possible.

Ritual purity must be distinguished from moral
sanctity. The latter belongs to man as a person. The
believing Israelite felt obligated to be irreproachable
in thought and in action in such a way that God's
sanctity became his example and norm: "Be holy, for
I am holy" (cf. Lev. 11:44; 19:2; 20:26 and Mt. 5:48).
Ritual sanctity is an obligation imposed on man by
the Old Covenant. Deep Old Testament conviction
of God's holiness is shown in the demand that man
be irreproachable and spotless even in his physical
life.

This striving for the greatest possible ritual perfection can be called asceticism, according to our definition given earlier. We prefer to call this cultual
asceticism; Levitical rules of purity are an example
of this type. The idea and its concrete forms is a
product of its time and environment even for Israel.
In the magic way of thinking of the man in the old
East, there was a certain territory that was taboo
for him, where he ought not enter because it was
filled with dangerous powers and exclusively re-
served for the deity. Violation of this rule prevented
one from contact with the deity. To protect this
divine domain and the individual person himself
certain practices which we consider typical of cultual

asceticism came into being. Israel however has special interpretations; these were the result of a gradual transformation under the guidance of the authentic Yahwist faith.

Cultual asceticism is naturally restricted to the stage of the Old Covenant. The New Covenant is characteristically the "end time." This is an eternal and immutable Covenant. The whole of human existence — even its bodily aspect — is characterized by the domination of the pneuma which gives the incorruptible life of the risen Lord. Human bodiliness in the New Covenant is sanctified through the saving action of the Spirit of the Lord.

Several other ascetic practices of renouncing the world are mentioned in the Bible, such as those of the so-called Nazarites — desert life, poverty, sexual abstinence, fasting and almsgiving. Their common inspirational source is the desire to manifest a firm faith in the historical reality of the saving God. In the New Covenant, faith must be practiced in the end time. The Old Covenant is a determined struggle toward the ultimate consequences of the Yahwist faith in a historical saving God for all mankind.

This last aspect — as regards asceticism — has impressed a special character on the Bible. After twenty centuries of Christianity we can still readily understand that the old Israel did not casually accept its faith in the historical saving God. The Old Testament is an impressive testimony of Israel's awareness that it is a sinful people. In it we read

about a national hereditary sin. The story is striking
because of the intensity with which — according
to the Sacred Books — the saving God showed himself to be insulted by Israel's refusal, so shortly after
the Covenant was established, to continue in historical communion of life with him. He rejects the
people which at the time of entering upon the
Covenant he had declared to be "his" people (cf. Ex.
19:4-6; 20:2): "Then the Lord said to Moses: Go
down; for **your** people, whom you brought out of
the land of Egypt, have corrupted themselves . . .
But Moses besought the Lord his God, and said: O
Lord, why does thy wrath burn against **thy** people,
whom thou hast brought forth out of the land of
Egypt with greater power and with a mighty hand?
. . . Repent of this evil against **thy** people . . . And
the Lord repented of the evil which he thought to
do to **his** people" (Ex. 32).

This sin was so deeply rooted in Israel that it was
considered a national heritage as far back as the
time of the desert (cf. Deut. 9:7; 10:5). According
to Israel's own conscience, it was always the same
sin: they behaved toward Yahweh as toward an un-
historical god of nature. For this reason they
described the sin in the desert as the sin of the
golden calf (Ex. 32).

The following paragraphs attempt to describe more
of the historical circumstances in which revelation
developed, and the consequent biblical asceticism
of "renouncing the world" which ensued from these.

1. The religions of nature in sedentary Canaan

The time when the tribes of Israel ended their journey of forty years in the desert and settled in Canaan was decisively important for the development of the Yahwist faith. To explain this it is necessary to make a comparison between the ancient Yahwism of nomadic Israel and the religion of Canaan, which offered Israel the model of a sedentary life.

Yahwism was really a faith of nomadic shepherds. Their God was a nomadic God. He had "guided" his chosen people from Egypt through the desert, and a cloud had been the sign of his presence: "And the Lord went before them by day in a pillar of cloud to lead them along the way, and by night in a pillar of fire to give them light, that they might travel by day and by night; the pillar of cloud by day and the pillar of fire by night did not depart from before the people" (Ex. 13:21-22; 14:19b, 20, 24; cf. Num. 14:14). The Ark of the Covenant, a visible sign of the divine presence in the midst of his people (Ex. 25:22; cf. 1 Sam. 4:4; 2 Sam. 6:2 etc.) functioned as a "guide" (cf. Num. 10:33; Jos. 3-4). As Yahweh was considered a "God of war" (Ex. 15:3-15; 14:14, 25; Num. 21:14; Judg. 7:2), the Ark was a palladium: "And whenever the ark set out, Moses said: Arise, O Lord, and let thy enemies be scattered, and let them that hate thee flee before thee. And when it rested, he said: Return, O Lord, to the ten thousand thousands of Israel" (Num. 10:35-36; Ps. 68:2; Jos. 6 etc.).

The nomadic character of their God was stressed

even more by his covenant. This was not based on a community of territory or of blood, but on the sovereign will of God, who chose for himself one people among all the peoples of the earth. It was characterized by personal relationship based on personal surrender. Consequently, its norms were not ritualistic but moral.

These moral demands were really customs and usages in which a nomadic community expressed and safeguarded its feeling of solidarity. By them Israel expressed the belief that their nomadic God safeguarded the people he had called into existence (cf. Deut. 32:6; Ex. 15:16; Is. 43:1, 15). He is not the God of "a crowd," but of "a people." The nomadic character of Yahwism was further emphasized by Israel's long sojourn in the desert.

We know very little about the cult used during this desert period. Probably there was no extensive calendar of feasts, nor a developed ritual of sacrifices (cf. Amos 5:25). Other than offering the firstlings of the flocks, customary among all nomads (Ex. 13:12; 3:4, 19), there seem to have been sacrifices only on special occasions, such as the entering upon of the Covenant near Sinai (Ex. 24:4 ff.). The Ark of the Covenant as the throne of Yahweh in the tent of revelation probably was the center of the cult, in accord with the life in the desert.

The religion of Canaan however was a religion of settled farmers. They were convinced that human existence depends entirely on the fertility of the soil. Their great obsession therefore was to gain control over and to dominate the many uncertain factors which influence fertility. All these factors were "baals" or "lords" for the Canaanite farmer. First there was the local deity, the god of the field, whom he had to placate by means of special rites. Next there were the baals of the cosmic powers, who also influenced fertility: the baal of the water below and of the water in heaven, the baal of the growth of the crops, the baals of the winds, the dew, etc.; there were also the different baals of the changing seasons. Some of these considered others to be implacable enemies, and the war they waged among themselves was in last resort a war between death, night and chaos on the one hand, and life, day and cosmos on the other. The vicissitudes of the gods in their world, as described in myths, were the universal pattern according to which all things on earth, social as well as religious, were modeled. What happened in the world of the gods set the pattern for what took place in the visible world. Conscious of this dependence, the Canaanite farmer was very much interested in maintaining harmony with the world of the gods.

In their pantheon there was also a certain hierarchy. At the top was the rather vague and passive figure of El, the supreme god who rules over gods and men. His wife was Ashera, originally a mother-goddess, but in practice she was usually considered the goddess of the growth of plants, and therefore the female partner of Baal. Her symbol was the

sacred pole (called "ashera") next to the altar (cf.
Judg. 6:25, 26, 28, 30; 1 Kings 14:15; 16:33 etc.).
Among their numerous children was Hadad, their
son (or grandson), most important because of his
great influence on fertility. Since he was the god
who controlled the rain needed for plant growth, he
was considered to be **the** Baal. Hadad's real wife
was Anath, infrequently mentioned in the Old Testament. She was the goddess of love and war. Finally
we must mention the Semitic goddess of vegetation
worshiped almost everywhere in the Near East:
Ashtarte, who according to the Old Testament was
especially venerated in Sidon (cf. 1 Kings, 11:5, 33;
2 Kings 23:12-13). Even in ancient times it seems
uncertain just who was Baal's wife: according to Ras
Shamra it was Anath; according to the Canaanites
of the Old Testament it probably was Ashtarte (cf.
Judg. 2:13; 10:6; 1 Sam. 7:14; 12:10); according
to Jezebel of Tyrus it was Asherah (cf. 1 Kings 18:19).

From this we may surmise that the local religion
really made no moral, only ritual demands. Rites,
performed in a magic way, were necessary to ensure
harmony between the earthly and the godly world.
They were celebrated especially on high places in
the open air, the so-called "sacrificial heights," found
near most Canaanite towns. Especially characteristic
of this agrarian cult of the Baals were human
sacrifices and erotic rites.

Human sacrifices were based on a deeply religious
sentiment: by offering to a god the first and the
best things before enjoying the rest themselves,

people expressed their recognition of the god's sovereign rights to the produce of life. The idea of the sacrifice of firstlings is also known in the Bible, but this demands a ransom for the human male firstborn; instead of the child, an animal must be sacrificed (cf. Ex. 34:19-20; cf. 13:2, 13; Lk. 2:22-24). The Canaanites, at least in certain times and places, put this idea into practice by sacrificing their firstborn males to Baal. Probably these were originally "foundation-sacrifices," which in ancient times dedicated new fields and later also new houses to the honor of the baal. A child was placed beneath the base of the wall, usually the threshold, or sometimes in the middle of the room, walled in or enclosed in a jar (1 Kings 16:34; cf. Jos. 6:26). Later on human beings were also evidently sacrificed to allay calamities of nature or military defeat. Thus the Bible tells about the shepherd-king Mesha, king of Moab (4 Kings 3:27): when he made his last stand at Kir Carsheth, surrounded and pressed by enemies, "he took his eldest son who was to reign in his stead, and offered him for a burnt offering upon the wall."

According to the Bible, it seems that the sacrifice of babies to Moloch was associated with this practice. Moloch, called by the Greeks **Khronos,** evidently is identical with the Phenician Baal.[6] The cult of Moloch, already known in the third millennium in Mesopotamia, must have flourished among the Canaanites and the Phoenicians. It is probable that the Kidron valley was a very old site of this cult of

Moloch (cf. 2 Chron. 28:2-4; 2 Kings 16:3-4). Moloch was a chthonian deity whose realm was below the earth; he caused wars and epidemics to populate his kingdom. To pacify him people sent him selected victims, especially young children. This is what we know about the cult of Moloch. The Biblical expression for this sacrifice is ". . . to devote them by fire to Moloch" — in other words, to burn them (cf. Lev. 18:21; 2 Kings 23:10; Jer. 32:35). Exactly what this meant may perhaps be concluded from a description which Diodorus of Sicily has given us about a statue of the Mili Khronos at Carthage. "The Carthagenians had a brass statue of Khronos, who kept his hands stretched out toward the earth with the palms turned up and so the child placed upon them rolled off and fell into a pit filled with fire." Thus we get an idea about the furnace called the Topeth in the valley of Gehenna (cf. Jer. 7:31) and we understand how the Bible gave the name "gehenna" to the hell of the eschatological time and pictured it as a fire in which the damned are burning.

Erotic rites were intended to foster fertility and productivity of fields, cattle and man. The idea underlying them is that the mystery of vegetal growth and human fertility are somehow connected: the cycle of human birth, growth and decay is a living reflection of the cycle of vegetal growth; the same life pulses in both. Man thus becomes part of nature in its seasons, its cycle of sowing and harvesting, of dying and acquiring new life.

In his struggle to subdue the soil and to make it fertile, the Canaanite farmer knew no better means than to gear his own life to the living rhythm of the vegetal process of growing. That is why in the baal rites the feminine element plays such an important role. In such a milieu this is easy to understand, because the motherly womb of woman in its creative fertility has an obvious parallel with the lifegiving womb of the fields.

During the religious feasts mythological stories were probably dramatized and some at least of these dramatizations must have been as frankly erotic as the myths themselves. This would especially have been the case with the feast of spring, which the people considered to be the mating time of the goddess of fertility (mother earth represented by a sacred prostitute) with her baal, the god of rain and vegetal growth.

In any case, sacred prostitution of men as well as of women was widely practiced (cf. Deut. 23:18-19). In Phoenecia, besides the priests, male and female prostitutes frequently belonged to the temple. They devoted themselves to the service of Ashtarte, the goddess of fertility. Sacred prostitution was originally practiced in the open air to make it more effective. This was the case in the hill shrines and in Canaanite shrines as well.

Thus in Israel and Canaan, we see two types of culture and two corresponding religions. We can surmise the difficulties of the Israelites as they settled to sedentary life in Canaan.

2. Yahwism "baalized"

The first thing that strikes us is the social dislocation — one might say upheaval — caused by the change from a nomadic to a sedentary life. The routine of a settled farmer or citizen is entirely different from free nomadic wandering in the desert. The farmer does not know the safety of the closed family community or clan, each with its own household economy, its own system of morals and customs. A sedentary culture has a centralized government apparatus with a hierarchy of officials, a specialized state economy with different branches, such as artisans, officials, soldiers, traders. This pattern of life, being more variegated, offers greater possibilities of material affluence; but it also makes greater moral demands on man. Here he enjoys the profits of material progress, such as a certain refinement of life and easier customs; but he is also exposed to accompanying dangers — luxury, avarice, unjustice, moral decay.

The extent to which this was the case with Israel has been described for us, and in no uncertain language, by the prophets. We hear their reproaches: "Woe to those who lie upon beds of ivory, and stretch themselves upon their couches, and eat lambs from the flock, and calves from the midst of the stall; who sing idle songs to the sound of the harp, and like David invent for themselves instruments of music; who drink wine in bowls, and anoint themselves with the finest oils, but are not grieved over the ruin of Joseph" (Amos 6:4-6; cf. 3:15). We

hear their threats: "Hear this, you who trample upon
the needy, and bring the poor of the land to an end,
saying: When will the new moon be over, that we
may sell grain? And the sabbath, that we may offer
for sale, that we may make the ephah small and the
shekel great, and deal deceitful with false balances,
that we may buy the poor for silver and the needy
for a pair of sandals, and sell the refuse of the wheat"
(Amos 8:4-6; cf. 2:6, 8; 5:11-12; Is. 1:17, 23; 3:14).
To the well-fed egoistic women of Samaria they
say: "Hear this word, you cows of Bashan, who
are in the mountains of Samaria, who oppress the
poor, who crush the needy, who say to their husbands:
Bring, that we may drink" (Amos 4:1; cf. Is. 3:16-24;
32:9-14). To those who carouse they say: "Woe to
those who rise early in the morning, that they may
run after strong drink, who tarry late in the evening
till wine inflames them! They have lyre and harp,
timbrel and flute and wine at their feasts; but they
do not regard the deeds of the Lord, or see the
work of his hands" (Is. 5:11-12).

Threat of social dislocation was a disquieting
reality for Israel; the very existence of the "people"
living in accord with the Yahwist faith was en-
dangered: in the Covenant Yahweh had told them
he did not choose to rule a "crowd" but a community.

To understand how this change to sedentary life,
with all the risks involved, took place it is important
to consider the geographical features of the country.
These were very unfavorable for the formation of a
firm political unity. In this regard Canaan differed

considerably from the surrounding lands. In the
time of the patriarchs (about 1900-1700) and even
in the 13th century a solidly organized state was
still unknown. To the east of the river Jordan the
monarchies of Edom, Moab and Ammon were already in existence (cf. Num. 21); in Canaan there
were only city states, each with its own king (cf.
Jos. 12). This naturally had a great influence on the
feasibility of Israel's plans to conquer the country,
and consequently on the further history of Israel.

Although the book of Joshua gives an idealized
description of the occupation of the country, the
Book of Judges shows a more objective version. The
occupation actually was not accomplished at a fast
tempo; and, after all, it was restricted to four en-
claves. The tribes of Ruben, Gad and East Manasseh
settled in a long strip of country in eastern Jordania,
from the Dead Sea on the south to the Sea of
Chinnereth on the north. The tribes of Ephraim and
West Manasseh settled to the west of the Jordan,
their territory bordering the plain of Israel on the
north and the cities of Jerusalem, Gezer, Libnah
and Lachish on the south (Jos. 16 and 17). The
tribes of Judah, Simeon (cf. Jos. 14; 15; 19; Judges
1) and Benjamin (Jos. 18:11-28) settled in the wide
Negeb in the south. The other tribes settled in the
Galilean hill country in the north (cf. Jos. 16-19).
The fact that the chosen people, from a territorial
point of view, did not form one coherent unit made
them vulnerable to aggression of surrounding peoples and bands of roaming plunderers. The period

which so often demanded recourse to born leaders is called the period of the Judges. Gradually however, especially under Philistine pressure, the Israelites more and more felt the absolute need for a central government, and changed to a monarchy (cf. 1 Sam. 8:5).

The isolated existence of the several Israelitic groups was not conducive to banishment of a tribal mentality. The case of "Shechem" is probably an example. The conquest of Shechem is not mentioned anywhere. This can be explained by supposing that it was inhabited by Hebrews who had never been in Egypt and who had never had the experiences of the other Hebrews. Or perhaps they were Hebrews who (about 1550 B.C. when the Hyksos were expelled) had already gone from Egypt and had settled in Canaan. This clan mentality greatly influenced later history of Israel.[7]

Moreover there was a difference in the situation of the northern and the southern tribes: for a long time the latter were still able to lead their familiar nomadic life in the Negeb desert; the northern tribes however were much more exposed to the influences and the threats of the aboriginal population of Canaan, with whom they had much closer contact. The song of Deborah (Judg. 5), which celebrates the union of the Israelitic tribes but omits Judah and Simeon, gives us an inkling of a cleft between North and South. In the beginning Judah played a small role in the national history; but its numbers gradually increased, due to an admixture of

many non-Israelitic elements. It eventually acquired
such a predominant position that a man from Judah,
David, was able to impose himself as the king of
all Israel. But even his forceful personality was unable to close the breach between North and South.
Thus the northern tribes, after the episode of Ab-
salom, came to David to complain: "Why have our
brethren the men of Judah stolen you away, and
brought the king and his household over the Jordan,
and all David's men with him? All the men of Judah
answered the men of Israel: Because the king is near
of kin to us. Why then are you angry about this
matter? Have we eaten at the king's expense? Or
has he given us any gift? And the men of Israel
answered the men of Judah: We have ten shares in
the king, and in David also we have more than you.
Why then did you despise us? Were we not the
first to speak of bringing back our king? But the
words of the men of Judah were fiercer than the
swords of the men of Israel" (2 Sam. 19:42-44). The
situation became so critical that during the reign
of David there was threat of a separation of the
northern tribes, stirred up by the agitator Sheba
(2 Sam. 20). Solomon moreover does not seem to
have followed an intelligent policy by favoring the
tribe of Judah, granting them freedom from taxes
(cf. 1 Kings 4). The latent tension between North
and South finally exploded into definite separation
when Solomon's son Rehoboam ascended the throne.
At a public meeting he antagonized the northern
tribes by stupid provocations (1 Kings 12:10 ff.).
Judah remained faithful to him, but the northern

sector chose Jeroboam, a man from the leading tribe of Ephraim, as a king.

The further history of the small kingdoms follows the history of their respective kings. In the southern kingdom the house of the Judean David was so closely connected with the royal throne in the "city of David" that his dynasty acquired more or less a complete stability there. The northern kingdom, because of its traditions and its situation, was not closely united with David's dynasty at Jerusalem. Unlike the southern kingdom, the North often changed dynasties and capitols. The greatest handicap for the northern kingdom was that it had no religious center to rival Jerusalem with its Ark of the Covenant. Two sanctuaries were founded by Jeroboam, at Dan and at Bethel, and they possessed a venerable tradition; but they were unable to inspire the people to unity and continuity to the extent that the real center of the worship of Yahweh in Jerusalem did. In fact, these sanctuaries gave rise to a degenerate Yahwism and finally caused the downfall of the kingdom (722). The southern kingdom was eventually unable to retard disintegration, political as well as religious. About 135 years later, in 586, Judah came to its end with the fall of Jerusalem. The captivity was necessary to break Israel's contact with the soil from which it had taken its pagan inspirations.

It is really not strange that the actual process of adaptation to sedentary life had such a strong in-

fluence on Yahwism. Their concrete model of a
sedentary religion was Canaan. The local worship
offered the Israelitic people many possibilities absent
in Yahwism. Their cult fitted in well with their
native eastern ideas about deities in close contact
with soil and blood. The erotic rites appealed to
their more primitive prurient instincts. The chosen
people's first contact with sedentary religiosity, even
before they entered Canaan, resulted in their seduction by Moabitic women, followed by worship of the
women's "baal of the abyss" (Num. 25:1 ff.). Once
they settled in the country, their conduct is described
in the Bible as follows: "They forsook the Lord, and
served the Baals and the Ashtaroth" (Judg. 2:11, 13;
3:7; 10:6). This will be the chief complaint during the
rest of Israel's history, until the time of captivity.
This fact found expression in the concept of the
national hereditary sin of Israel (Ex. 32-33). True
religious values and a real moral consciousness de-
generated into a mentality of magic accommodating
itself to pagan rites.

Besides this cultural prostitution, the Israelites often
followed the barbarous Canaanite custom of human
sacrifice. At the time of the prophet Micah there
seems to have been a number of pietistic Israelites
who naively asked themselves whether the sacrifice
of the first born might not perhaps also be the normal
ritual demand of their own God (6:7). In the explanation why Israel is punished by exile in Assyria (722)
we read that "they burned their sons and their
daughters as offerings" (2 Kings 17:17). In Judah

we hear about Ahab (736-716) that "he burned incense in the valley of the son of Hinnom, and burned his sons as an offering, according to the abominable practices of the nations whom the Lord drove out before the people of Israel" (2 Chron. 28:2-4; 2 Kings 16:3-4). We read how Manasseh, king of Judah (687-642), continued this practice, perhaps abolished by Hezekiah (716-687). Even after the pious Josiah of Judah (640-609) had wiped them out (2 Kings 23:10), these customs returned (Jer. 7:30-31; 19:5; 32:35; Ezek. 16:20-21; 20:31; 23:37, 39; Is. 57:9), in spite of Deuteronomic reaction (Deut. 12:31; 18:10-12). The priestly tradition pronounces its condemnation of these wicked practices (Lev. 18:21) and introduces capital punishment for this crime (Lev. 20:2-5).

Judging from first impressions, one might be inclined to ask if Israel completely abandoned Yahweh in Canaan. This evidently never happened. In their official professions of faith the people remained steadfast in acknowledging Yahweh as the only and incomparable God, highly exalted above any baal. In everyday practice however, they had come to consider the Canaanite baal a factor too important to neglect in the economic development of agriculture. Gradually it was to become an explicit point of faith that it was precisely Yahweh, their nomadic God, who had entire and exclusive dominion over the mysterious powers of the earth. Fertility had to be stripped of the idea of sexuality and considered a gracious gift of Yahweh.

In this regard, a noteworthy fact has come to light. Excavations[8] show that Israel evidently never made a male representation of Yahweh, even though this would have been logical, considering the many baal statues they had seen. It is probable that the statues of a young bull at Dan and Bethel, covered with gold and silver (1 Kings 12:28-38), originally a popular symbol of the god of fertility, really were intended as a kind of pedestal for the invisible Yahweh, not however as a representation of Yahweh himself. But it must have been difficult for the common people to keep this distinction well in mind; they could very well have worshiped them as "your gods, O Israel, who brought you up out of the land of Egypt" (1 Kings 12:28; cf. Ex. 32:4, 8 and Hos. 8:5; 13:2), therefore they might have considered them a real representation of Yahweh. It seems probable that from the time of the Judges many were irresistibly drawn to practices in which Yahweh was reduced to the status of just another god of nature, a baal, from whom fertility could be extorted by magic.

As long as this attitude was not formulated into an explicit confession of faith, it was difficult to counteract. But when the kings cooperated, it became official. It is tragic that the Israelitic kings — beginning with Solomon (1 Kings 11) and reaching a dramatic height under Ahab in the North (1 Kings 16:30 ff.) and Manasseh in the South (2 Kings 21:1-17) — led the chosen people to their downfall. They actually provoked and made possible an open frontal attack against the "baalization" of Yahwism.

3. Back to the desert

In trying to discover a reason why the authentic
practice of Yahwism suffered we find it necessary
to look back to the sources, and especially to the
northern kingdom, where the wicked influence of
Canaan was strongest. "When Israel was a child,
I loved him, and out of Egypt I called my son.
The more I called them, the more they went from
me; they kept sacrificing to the Baals, and burning
incense to idols" (Hos. 11:1); "Like the first fruit on
the fig tree, in its first season, I saw your fathers.
But they came to Baal-peor, (cf. Num. 25), and
consecrated themselves to shame, and became de-
testable like the thing they loved!" (Hos. 9:10); "It
was I who knew you in the wilderness, in the land
of drought; but when they had fed to the full, they
were filled,' and their heart was lifted up; therefore
they forgot me!" (Hos. 13:5). These are the prophet
Hosea's complaints of a rejected love; he preached in
the northern kingdom between 750 and 735, (cf.
also Micah 6:2 ff.; 7:14 ff.). But Hosea continues:
". . . says the Lord . . . I will allure her (i.e. Israel),
and bring her into the wilderness, and speak tenderly
to her . . . And in that day, says the Lord, you will
call me: My husband, and no longer will you call
me my baal . . . And I will betroth you to me for
ever; I will betroth you to me . . ." (Hos. 2:16 ff.).
Amos — though born in Judah preached in the
northern kingdom about 750 — recalls Yahweh's
solicitude in the desert. "Also I brought you up out
of the land of Egypt, and led you forty years in the
wilderness, to possess the land of the Amorite" (2:10).

For Isaiah and his followers, just as for Hosea
(2:16 ff.) the time of the desert is to return and
Israel's redemption will be a second exodus: "Therefore thus says the Lord, the Lord of hosts: O my
people, who dwell in Zion, be not afraid of the
Assyrians when they smite with the rod and lift
their staff against you as the Egyptians did. For in
a very little while my indignation will come to an
end, and my anger will be directed to their destruction. And the Lord of hosts will wield against them
a scourge, as when he smote Midian at the rock of
Oreb (cf. Judg. 7:25); and his rod will be over the
sea, and he will lift it as he did in Egypt. And in
that day his burden will depart from your shoulder,
and his yoke will be destroyed from your neck"
(10:24-27; cf. 11:15-16). The anonymous prophet of
the Book of Consolation (Is. 40-55) predicts that the
Babylonian exiles will return to Palestine; there will
be a new exodus, with Yahweh in the lead: "Thus
says the Lord, who makes a way in the sea (Ex.
14:21-29), a path in the mighty waters, who brings
forth chariot and horse, army and warrior; they lie
down and cannot rise, they are extinguished,
quenched like a wick: Remember not the former
things, nor consider the things of old. Behold, I
am doing a new thing; now it springs forth, do you
not perceive it? I will make a way in the wilderness
and rivers in the desert. The wild beasts will honor
me, the jackals and the ostriches; for I give water
in the wilderness, rivers in the desert, to give drink
to my chosen people, the people whom I formed for
myself that they might declare my praise" (43:16-21;
cf. 40:3-5; 48:21; 51-10; 52:11-12 and 63:11-14).

Jeremiah sees the desert as a remembrance of an exemplary beginning (2:1-3) and as a promise of future salvation: "At that time, says the Lord, I will be the God of all the families of Israel, and they shall be my people. Thus says the Lord: The people who survived the sword found grace in the wilderness; when Israel sought for rest, the Lord appeared to him from afar" (31:1-2).

It is natural that the prophets look back to the time of the desert; the foundations of Yahwism were laid in this period. But man is often too inclined to idealize the past, especially if there is much to be criticized in the present. Some of the Israelites definitely disliked or even absolutely abhorred city culture; they considered the decay of religious life in the world due to the rise and progress of a sedentary culture. Obviously they had the experiences in Canaan in mind; this is evident from the curse of Ham, whom the Biblical writer presents as the forefather of the Canaanites (cf. Gen. 9:20-27). There was also a group of historians who, because of their tragic experiences in Israel, thought that an earthly kingship, "like all the nations" have, is a rejection of Yahweh himself as king (2 Sam. 8:5-7). They nostalgically remembered Yahweh's exclusive leadership of the community when the people roamed in the desert.

This limited reaction against the pagan influence of Canaan led to a radical rejection of all sedentary culture. The Bible tells us about the Rechabites — originally a group of nomadic inhabitants of the

desert, akin to the Kenites (cf. 1 Chron. 2:55) — who
cultivated an ideal of the nomadic life such as Israel
led when called by Yahweh (cf. Jer. 35).

There seems to have been a definite relationship
between all the different groups we have mentioned.
They were longing for a religious ideal and for the
nomadic way of life that went with it. We read
that Jehonadab, founder of the Rechabites, helped
Jehu (842-815) extirpate the house of Ahab and the
baal cult from the northern kingdom (2 Kings 10:15
ff.). Shortly before this, but during Ahab's reign,
the leader of the struggle for the orthodox Yahwist
cult was the famous Elijah, whose memory lived for
posterity in a cycle of legendary stories (1 Kings
17:1-19, 21; 21:17-28; 2 Kings 1:2; 2:12). The narra-
tive of his journey to Horeb the holy mountain
depicts him as a real "man of the desert," a second
Moses (1 Kings 19:1-21; cf. Mt. 17:1-9 par.). According to the Bible, Elijah was a **nabi** (1 Kings 18:22, 39).
This means that he belonged to a class of charis-
matics whose chief task, even during the time of
the kings, was to fight for the maintenance of
Yahweh's sovereign leadership according to the strict
rules of Yahwism. They played their role when
Israel had its first king (cf. 1 Sam. 10:1; 16:1; cf.
1 Sam. 3:20, where Samuel too is called **nabi**). After
the schism they supervised the many dynastic
changes in the northern kingdom (1 Kings 11:29-39;
16:1-7; 19:16; 2 Kings 9:1 ff.), seemingly bringing
it back to a status more in conformity with the old
Yahwist ideal of charismatic leadership. It is there-

fore quite probable that these different circles influenced one another.

Though several of these **nabis** led a nomadic life (Elijah, Elisha, Samuel), they nevertheless did not definitively raise this way of life to a religious ideal; nor were the writing prophets able to do this. Only the Rechabites were successful — and they operated in too absolute a manner. Their period of influence came much later (in the first centuries B.C. and A.D.) in the community of Qumran.[9] The writing prophets and the **nabis** were not enemies of sedentary culture. This is evident from **nabi** interventions in the affairs of the kings, which prove that they did not deem the kingship as such incompatible with Yahwism. Among the writing prophets, for example, Isaiah declares agriculture to be an art taught by Yahweh (28:23-29).

Yet the desert had a special attraction for the Biblical traditions of faith. It is essentially "a land of deserts and pits, a land of drought and deep darkness, a land that none passes through, where no man dwells" (Jer. 2:6). Only when invited by God and when entirely dependent upon him can one live there. Hence the desert, according to the Bible, is the special place for purest love, where lovers could associate in a most exclusive way (cf. Hos. 2:16; Jer. 2:2). This is the fundamental idea expressed by the writer of the book of Deuteronomy. Moses' farewell speech to the chosen people, delivered in the fields of Moab, reminds the people of Yahweh's love for them and of his desire to be loved by them.

"It was not because you were more in number than
any other people that the Lord set his love upon you
and chose you, for you were the fewest of all peoples;
but it is because the Lord loves you, and is keeping
the oath which he swore to your fathers, that the
Lord loved you" (Deut. 7:7-8); "The Lord set his
heart in love upon your fathers and chose their
descendants after them, you above all peoples"
(10:15); "The Lord your God would not hearken to
Balaam, but the Lord your God turned the curse
into a blessing for you, because the Lord your God
loved you" (23:6); "And because he loved your fathers
and chose their descendants after them . . . know
therefore this day, and lay it to your heart, that the
Lord is God in heaven above and on the earth
beneath; there is no other" (4:35 ff.); "You shall
therefore love the Lord your God, and keep his
charge, his statutes, his ordinances, and his commandments always" (11:1). Israel dares not listen
to false prophets and dreamers "for the Lord your
God is testing you, to know whether you love the
Lord your God with all your soul" (13:4); "Hear, O
Israel: the Lord our God is one Lord; and you
shall love the Lord your God with all your heart,
and with all your soul, and with all your might"
(6:4-5).

Israel is united to Yahweh in a personal bond of
love. It does not face the dark powers of nature,
controllable by magic techniques. The Deuteronomic
word of Moses is a passionate appeal to the hearts
of the chosen people, pleading that they show their

love by keeping Yahweh's commands. The exhorting style of the book is typical of this writer. It is an insistent prophetic call: "And these words which I command you this day shall be (written) upon your heart; and you shall teach them diligently to your children, and shall talk of them when you sit in your house, and when you walk by the way, and when you lie down, and when you rise. And you shall bind them as a sign upon your hand, and they shall be as frontlets between your eyes. And you shall write them on the doorposts of your house and on your gates" (6:6-9). He who loves knows deep in his heart how he can please his beloved: "For this commandment which I command you this day is not too hard for you, neither is it far off. It is not in heaven, that you shall say: Who will go up for us to heaven, and bring it to us, that we may hear it and do it? Neither is it beyond the sea, that you should say: Who will go over the sea for us and bring it to us, that we may hear it and do it? But the word is very near you: it is in your mouth and in your heart, so that you can do it" (30:11-14).

This is the "desert ideal" for which the people of God must strive. It does not imply that they must lead a nomadic life again; it means that they should be reinspired by the spirituality characteristic of the time in the desert when they lived under the direct leadership of the God of the Covenant.

This ideal — the perfect bond of love with the historically saving God — was actually never entirely realized in the Old Covenant. Even the former time of the desert was only its pale foreshadowing. But the saving God always called it to mind so that it might finally be realized in the New Covenant. He will then lead his bride into the desert again where he will speak to her heart; he will again betroth himself to her, this time for ever (cf. Hos. 2:16, 21 and the other prophets quoted above).

4. Asceticism which "renounces the world"

Biblical asceticism has no desire to impose upon all the people of God a way of life without a fixed dwelling place or without any of the benefits of a sedentary culture. But it does preach this way of living as an ideal for some individuals, either during their whole life or for a certain time. This is made evident by the following examples.

(a) We find an ancient practice of renouncing the world codified in the book of Numbers (6:1-21) and adapted to the Levitic ritual; it is called **Nazarism.** A Nazarite was a person especially dedicated to God. In the early days of Israel this was specifically a commitment to a holy war (cf. Samson, Judg. 13:5). Warriors then wore long hair (cf. Judg. 5:2 and Deut. 32:2). Hence it was natural that unshorn locks became the symbol of a warrior in a holy war (Judg. 13:5, 7; 16:17). It appears that this type of Nazarism eventually was spiritualized (cf. Amos 2:11 ff.) and sublimated into a complete dedication to the service of God in the temple (cf. 1 Sam. 1:11). Further development naturally made similar rules (cf. Num. 6:1-21) compulsory also for priests (cf. Lev. 21:1; 6:11). Moreover we find a development from charismatic Nazarism as a lasting state of life (Judg. 13:4-5, 7, 13-14; Amos 2:11-12) to a temporary, more ascetic vow (Num. 6:1-21; 1 Macc. 3:49; Acts 18:18; 21:23).

The three duties a Nazarite took upon himself according to the law (Num. 1-21) are typical instances of his spirituality. His long hair, not to be touched by scissors, (Num. 6:5), was distinctive of the warrior in God's holy war, well understood in those days (cf. above); consequently, it designated all who wished to dedicate themselves especially to the service of Yahweh (cf. Amos 2:11-12; 1 Sam. 1:11; Num. 6:9, 18; Deut. 14:1-2; Lev. 21:5-6; Acts 18:18). The duty to shun all contact with a corpse (Num. 6:6-7) arises from the Biblical conviction that all life belongs to Yahweh. Whatever in any way connotes death is unclean and unholy, because it is incompatible with Yahweh, who is a living God. Nazarite dedication to the living God obtains a special contemporary accent from a third duty, abstention from all the fruits of the vine (Num. 6:3-4; Amos 2:11-12; cf. Judg. 13:4, 7, 13-14). Israel considered viniculture a feature of the Canaanite civilization, so harmful to the true religious life of Yahwism (cf. Gen. 9:20-27 and Jer. 35). Nazarism ultimately became a defense of belief in Yahweh as the historical God of salvation.

The historical situation helps us understand how Israel could come to this asceticism of world-renunciation. But at the same time it shows that this

form was entirely time-bound. We may also conclude
that Nazarism developed more spiritualized insights;
it made possible a definite advance from a purely
cultual to a mystical asceticism.

(b) Basic Yahwism found special expression in
the **community of Levites.**[10] Biblical tradition shows
the evolution of this group. In the older writings
we find them an ethnic unit: they are one of the
twelve tribes of Israel. Their tribal forefather is
Levi, the third son Jacob and Leah (Gen. 29:34).
In the blessing of Jacob (Gen. 49:1-27), usually considered one of the oldest texts in the Pentateuch,
Levi and Simeon are described as a pair of violent
brothers (Gen. 34). Jacob curses them by predicting:
"I will divide them in Jacob and scatter them in
Israel" (Gen. 49:7). Indeed, the tribe of Simeon
soon disappeared by being absorbed into the tribe
of Judah. The tribe of Levi did not receive its own
territory as an inheritance when Canaan was divided;
its members lived dispersed throughout the entire
Israelitic community. In the blessing of Moses
(Deut. 33:2-29), certainly of a later date (possibly
during the reign of Jeroboam of the North), the
tribe of Levi is praised for its religious work in
Israel (Deut. 33:8-11).

If we desire an explanation for these different eval-
uations of the Levites in Israel's traditions we must
trace the deeper motives involved. The blessing of
Moses may guide us: "And of Levi he (Moses) said:
Give to Levi thy Thummim, and thy Urim to thy godly
one, whom thou didst test at Massah, with whom thou

didst strive at the waters of Meribah; who said of
his father and mother: I regard them not; he dis-
owned his brothers, and ignored his children. For
they observe thy word, and kept thy covenant"
(Deut. 33:8-10). Among the different memories of
the desert recalled here (cf. Num. 20:1-13; 25:7-10)
— in our text the role of the Levites is not clearly
expressed — there is clear allusion to what we read
in Ex. 32:25-29: the attitude of the sons of Levi,
when all others debased themselves by worshiping
the golden calf (Ex. 32). "And when Moses saw that
the people had broken loose (for Aaron had let them
break loose, to their shame among their enemies),
then Moses stood in the gate of the camp and said:
Who is on the Lord's side? Come to me. And all
the sons of Levi gathered themselves together to
him. And he said to them: Thus says the Lord God
of Israel: Put every man his sword on his side, and
go to and fro from gate to gate throughout the
camp, and slay every man his brother, and every
man his companion, and every man his neighbor.
And the sons of Levi did according to the word of
Moses; and there fell of the people that day about
three thousand men. And Moses said: Today you
have ordained yourselves for the service of the Lord,
each one at the cost of his son and of his brother,
that he may bestow a blessing upon you this day"
(cf. Deut. 10:8-9).

These texts show how, in Israel's tradition, the
Levites developed from a profane clan (cf. Gen. 34;
49) to a religious confraternity. The decisive turning
point in this development is the time in the desert,

when they made themselves champions of pure
Covenant observance.

Biblical tradition is a living tradition. The Deuteronomic school sought inspiration for its theology
in the old mosaic faith; the priestly circles after the
exile also desired an improved edition of the mosaic
traditions thus far collected. Their theology is based
on the idea that the priesthood of Jerusalem is the
only lawful one. As a result, priests, like the
Levites, outside Jerusalem found themselves degraded
to lower functions. Lev. 8 (cf. Ex. 29) describes
the rites for the consecration of Aaron and his sons;
Num. 3:5-9 calls the Levites helpers of the priests:
"They shall perform duties for him (Aaron) and for
the whole congregation" in the care for all that is
necessary in the cult. In the same chapter of the
book of Numbers we read that the Levites occupied
a very special place within the community of the
children of Israel: "And the Lord said to Moses:
Behold, I have taken the Levites from among the
people of Israel instead of every first-born that opens
the womb among the people of Israel. The Levites
shall be mine, for all the first-born are mine; on
the day that I slew all the first-born in the land of
Egypt (Ex. 12:29-34), I consecrated for my own all
the first-born in Israel, both of man and of beast;
they shall be mine; I am the Lord." Thus the
Levites are consecrated to God as a replacement
for the first-born sons of Israel, who must always
be redeemed (cf. Num. 3:11-13, 40-51; 8:16 ff.; cf.
Ex. 13:11 ff.; 22:28-29; 34:19-20; Deut. 15:19-20).

The Bible explains the nature of persons and things from their names. This was also done in the case of Levi. The origin of his tribe is explained by the words of Leah, the wife whom Jacob preferred next to Rachel, when her third son was born: "Now this time my husband will be joined to me" (Gen. 34:29). The author here gives a popular etymology of the Hebrew verbal root **lawah,** which means "to accompany" — to adhere to, to cleave to. The priestly author uses this same word in his explanation of the Levites as a religious institution. When Yahweh charges Aaron and his son with responsibility for the fulfillment of their priestly function he adds: "And with you bring your brethren, also, the tribe of Levi, the tribe of your father, that they may join you, and minister to you while you and your sons . . ." (Num. 18:2, 4).

It is worthy of note that Scriptual tradition acknowledges both the profane and the religious origin of the Levites with regard to their place in the chosen people of God. Though especially attached to God, they never lose their ties with the world. The Deuteronomist says: "And if a Levite comes from any of your towns out of all Israel, where he lives — and he may come when he desires — to the place which the Lord will choose (the central sanctuary of cult in Jerusalem), then he may minister in the name of the Lord his God, like all his fellow-Levites who stand to minister there before the Lord. They shall have equal portions to eat, besides what he receives from the sale of his patrimony" (Deut. 18:6-8). And the priestly author speci-

fies further: "And the Lord said to Moses: This is
what pertains to the Levites: From twenty-five years
old and upward they shall go in to perform the work
in the service of the tent of meeting. And from the
age of fifty years they shall withdraw from the work
of the service and serve no more, but minister to
their brethren in the tent of meeting, to keep the
charge, and they shall do no service. Thus shall
you do to the Levites in assigning their duties"
(Num. 8:23-26). Thus the Levitic group within the
community of Israel became a living expression of
the ideal of the Covenant: to be **in** the world, but
not **of** the world. The real nature of Yahwism,
especially in its attempt to assimilate the earthly
values of culture, finds expression in the form of
the Levitic institute, whose origin derives from the
moment the Covenant was entered upon in the desert.

It is possible that the Levitic ideal to lead, as a
tribe without territory, a nomadic life within the
Israelitic community (cf. Deut. 10:8-9; Num. 18:20;
Gen. 49:7) can be partially explained from an inborn
inclination to this way of life. According to this
view, they agitated against lasting settlement of
the Hebrews in Egypt, which at times appeared
probable (cf. Gen. 47:27); they were the great pro-
moters of the exodus (the great Levitic leaders were
Moses and Aaron). They were the ones who kept
reminding the Hebrews that they were only **gerim**
(strangers) in Egypt (Gen. 15:13; Ex. 22:20; 23:9;
Lev. 19:34; Deut. 10:10; 23:8; cf. Acts 7:6-7). The
Bible uses this term to indicate that the patriarchal

way of life was only a **megoorim** (pilgrimage) (Gen. 17:8; 28:4; 36:7; 37:1; 47:9; Ex. 6:4). This mentality of being **gerim** — not only strangers, but people who had no desire to relinquish their nomadic nature even in Egypt — made the exodus possible.

The Bible illustrates Levitic spirituality in another way. In Num. 3:9 and 8:16 the Levites are called **netinim** — "given," or loaned to the priests. The same word is used to indicate a certain group of people returning from the Babylonian exile (cf. Ezra 2:43 and Neh. 11:3, 21). They and the descendants of the slaves of Solomon (Ezra 2:55; Neh. 11:3; cf. 1 Kings 9:20 ff.) performed lesser duties in the temple, such as hewing wood and carrying water. This function dates from the first period of Israel's residence in Canaan (Jos. 9). Within the sedentary Israelitic community the situation of these **netinim** had become a situation of **gerim,** because they were of Canaanite origin. Since the Levites were akin to that class of people they formed a link between the profane world of Canaan and the religious world of Yahweh.

The Levites kept aloof from agriculture and any other lucrative occupation in Canaan, such as the trades the chosen people adopted, especially during the reign of Solomon. Refusal of all possessions made them really poor and dependent on the charity of their compatriots (Deut. 14:27). The fact that they did not hesitate to break even their family bonds when defense of Yahwism required it (Deut. 33:8-11; Ex. 32:25-29; cf. Num. 25:7 ff., 10 ff.),

caused them to be orphans in the midst of the
chosen people. For the Levites there was literally
no other inheritance except Yahweh alone (Deut.
10:9). It was their vocation to show, by their way
of life, the special union between God and even the
humblest social classes: the paupers, the disinherited,
the widows and orphans who usually had no support
at all, the **gerim** (cf. Deut. 14:28-29; 26:12-13). In this
way Levitic spirituality served as the beginning of
the spirituality of the "poor of Yahweh" (cf. below
under c) and was its inspiring example. It is
natural that Biblical tradition considers the Levites
the divinely appointed spiritual leaders of the chosen
people (Deut. 31:9 ff.).

(c) It should be noted that a positive attitude
toward the world, and a simultaneous attitude of
renouncing it can both originate from belief that
man's existence really means identification with the
God of salvation in this world. **Material poverty** as
an ideal to be lived is another point of faith which
the Bible acquired only gradually. This religious
consciousness followed different roads in its development; we can perhaps distinguish various
phases.

(1) Originally, the Israelites and all ancient Semites were convinced that poverty was something to
be abhorred. Man seeks happiness; the Semites
could not conceive of any happiness beyond the
horizon of this material world. Poverty, for them,
is an infringement on human existence. Revelation

gave Israel no other ideal. The ideal could receive only new motivation.

The Covenant of Sinai, which Israel could thank for its existence as a people, also made demands on them. The God of the Covenant wished a "community" as his partner, not a "crowd." An expression of this religious consciousness is the social aspect of Israel's legislation. In fact, these laws are the typical customs and usages of a nomadic community, in which it expresses and safeguards its feeling of belonging together; this is transposed to a sedentary community situation along with attendent agricultural possessions. We read in the law: "When you reap your harvest in your field, and have forgotten a sheaf in the field, you shall not go back to get it; it shall be·for the sojourner, the fatherless, and the widow; that the Lord your God may bless you in all the work of your hands" (Deut. 24:19; Lev. 23:22). "When you beat your olive trees, you shall not go over the boughs again; it shall be for the sojourner, the fatherless, and the widow" (Deut. 24:20). "When you gather the grapes of your vineyard, you shall not glean it afterward; it shall be for the sojourner, the fatherless, and the widow" (Deut. 24:21; Lev. 19:10). "At the end of every three years you shall bring forth all the tithe of your produce in the same year, and lay it up within your towns; and the Levite, because he has no portion or inheritance with you, and the sojourner, the fatherless, and the widow, who are within your towns, shall come and eat and be filled" (Deut. 14:28-29; 26:12-13). The real prac-

tice of solidarity in the people of God demands
extreme consequences: "When you go into your
neighbor's vineyard, you may eat your fill of grapes,
as many as you wish, but you shall not put any in
your vessel. When you go into your neighbor's
standing grain, you may pluck the ears with your
hand, but you shall not put a sickle to your neighbor's
standing grain" (Deut. 23:25-26; cf. Mt. 12:1 and
par.). We must also include the laws about the
sabbatical year (Ex. 23:10-11; Lev. 25:2-7) and the
jubilee year (Lev. 25:8-17, 23, 55).

Though the population in Canaan must have been
chiefly agrarian, the laws of the Covenant do not
aim to exclude the population of the cities from this
Yahwist ideal: "You shall not oppress a hired servant
who is poor and needy; whether he is one of your
brethren or one of the sojourners, who are in your
land within your towns, you shall give him his hire
on the day he earns it, before the sun goes down"
(Deut. 24:14, 15). "You shall not pervert the justice
due to the sojourner or to the fatherless, or take a
widow's garment in pledge" (Deut. 24:17; cf. Ex.
22:20; Jer. 7:6; 22:3; Ex. 22:7, 29). "When a stranger
sojourns with you in your land, you shall not do
him wrong. The stranger who sojourns with you
shall be to you as the native among you, and you
shall love him as yourself; for you were strangers
in the land of Egypt; I am the Lord your God"
(Lev. 19:33-34). "And if your brother becomes poor,
and cannot maintain himself with you, you shall
maintain him; as a stranger and a sojourner he shall

live with you" (Lev. 25:35). "Cursed be he who per-
verts the justice due to the sojourner, the fatherless,
and the widow" (Deut. 27:19). "He (Yahweh) exe-
cutes justice to the fatherless and the widow, and
loves the sojourner, giving him food and clothing.
Love the sojourner therefore; for you were sojourners in the land of Egypt" (Deut. 10:18-19; Ps.
146:9; Mal. 3:5).

For the pious Israelite this was the way for
survival in Canaan — the ideal of solidarity dating
from their nomadic existence when they were entirely dependent on the providence of their nomadic
God. They had to bear in mind that — as Lev.
25:23 puts it very tersely — "the land is mine
(Yahweh's); for you (Israel) are strangers (**gerim**)
and sojourners with me" (cf. Ps. 39:19; 119:19; 1
Chron. 29:15; 1 Pet. 2:11).

The same principle is true for the New Covenant,
but here it is formulated in a more universal way:
"All the earth is mine" (Ex. 19:5; cf. Deut. 10:14;
Ps. 23:1; 49:12; Is. 66:1-2; Ps. 88:12; Jer. 5:24; 1 Cor.
10:26), and you are "strangers and sojourners" with
me (1 Pet. 2:21; cf. 2:9-10; Ex. 19:5-6). It is a new
Covenant rule that the social equilibrium of the
people of God may not be disturbed. The oldest
Christian community, according to Luke, is characterized by its brotherly unanimity (Acts 2:41; cf.
Gal. 2:9; Philem. 6; 1 Jn. 1:3, 6, 7); this manifested
itself in a communion of material goods, which
provided for the needs of the poor (Acts 2:44-45;
4:32-33). This common possession of material goods

however did not get beyond the experimental stage. It was natural in the first phase of the eager expectation of the parousia, but it could not be maintained as a general Christian way of life in the world.

Paul collected money in the pagan churches, and he repeatedly stressed the importance of combating social poverty in the mother church of Jerusalem (Rom. 15:25-28, 31; cf. Acts 24:17; 2 Cor. 8-9; Gal. 2:10; 6:6 etc.). Interchange of spiritual and material goods within the one community of love of the people of God should foster unity between the faithful who came from paganism and those who converted from Judaism. The people of God in the New Covenant must show by its actions that the Old Covenant expectations of salvation are now realized. In the early days brotherly love could still be restricted to one people or to those who lived nearby (cf. the Old Testament summation in Lev. 19 and 20). In the New Covenant however this restriction is radically changed (Mt. 5:44; 22:34-40; cf. Mk. 12:28-31; Lk. 10:25-28). The new people of God must show by its behavior that the saving love of God is now a world-wide reality which breaks through all boundaries: "There is neither Jew nor Greek, there is neither slave nor free, there is neither male nor female; for you are all one in Christ Jesus" (Gal. 3:28).

(2) According to Biblical revelation, poverty should not exist within the people of God or in the New Covenant; the religious faith of the New Covenant, compared with the Old, developed this point

to a greater degree as its concept of redemption became more profound.

The Sacred Books show an evolution in another direction, also related to the nature of revealed redemption. Originally, Israel's main concern was material welfare as a reward for faithfully keeping the Covenant. Poverty was a punishment for sin and therefore abominable. This view continued for a long time, as we can see in Job; he could not understand why his entire possessions and even his numerous children were taken from him, although he was unaware of any guilt.

A more realistic view of life easily showed that many people live in poverty and distress only because they are oppressed and exploited by the rich. All that is left for them is their right to the blessings the Covenant promised; these they hope to receive in the messianic time (Is. 11:4; Ps. 72:2; 37:11). The prophets considered this social disorder a consequence of the godless materialism to which people so easily fell victims in a sedentary civilization. As a consequence, in a too simple way, religious importance was ascribed to social position. Thus in Hosea (12:8-9) Ephraim, having grown rich by his trade could boast: "Ah, but I am rich, I have gained wealth for myself," but all his riches can never offset the guilt he has incurred. Yahweh is angry with those who say: "When will the new moon be over, that we may sell grain? And the sabbath, that we may offer wheat for sale, that we may make the ephah small and the shekel great, and deal deceit-

fully with false balances, that we may buy the poor
for silver and the needy for a pair of sandals, and
sell the refuse of the wheat?" (Am. 8:5-7) Yahweh
threatens the city (Jerusalem?) "whose rich men are
full of violence, whose inhabitants speak lies" (Mic.
6:12) and those "who devise wickedness and work
evil upon their beds. When the morning dawns, they
perform it, because it is in the power of their hand.
They covet fields, and seize them; and houses, and
take them away; they oppress a man and his house,
a man and his inheritance" (Mic. 2:1-3; cf. Is. 10:1-2).

From these texts it is evident that Yahweh is not
against any class of people as such, but against the
debased tendencies to which a privileged position
so easily leads. A broader view of the group which
we mentioned here, in a social as well as a religious
aspect, is given in the literature of the Psalms. The
people of whom they speak are men who really have
succeeded in life and who deem this sufficient
reason to consider themselves important. "They (the
sinners) have no pangs, their bodies are sound and
sleek. They are not in trouble as other men are;
they are not stricken like other men. Therefore pride
is their necklace; violence covers them as a garment.
Their eyes swell out with fatness, their hearts over-
flow with follies. They scoff and speak with malice;
loftily they threaten oppression. They set their
mouths against the heavens, and their tongue struts
through the earth. Therefore the people turn and
praise them, abundant waters are drained by them.
And they say: How can God know? Is there knowl-

edge in the Most High?" (Ps. 73:3-11; cf. Ps. 37; 22:8-9).

Yahweh's care for the poor can be fully explained by his will to redress the injustice done to them: "The Lord enters into judgment with elders and princes of his people: It is you who have devoured the vineyard, the spoil of the poor is in your houses. What do you mean by crushing my people, by grinding the face of the poor? says the Lord God of hosts" (Is. 3:14-15); "With righteousness he (the Messiah) shall judge the poor, and decide with equity for the meek of the earth" (Is. 11:4).

But the Bible does not stop here. Victims of social injustice enjoy the special preference of Yahweh; so will all whose life in the world seems a complete failure, like the sick, the prisoners, the dishonored, the childless. It is not their social situation as such that makes them Yahweh's favorites, but the fact that they are without any pretensions. They are understanding and considerate of their fellowmen, humble and unshakable in their blind confidence in God, their Savior in all kinds of distress. God is much more for these people than a powerful Savior: he is the God of salvation, full of goodness and mercy; and thus the God who forgives the repentant sinner. "For thus says the high and lofty One who inhabits eternity, whose name is Holy: I dwell in the high and holy place, and also with him who is of a contrite and humble spirit, to revive the spirit of the humble, and to revive the heart of the contrite" (Is. 57:15; cf. 66:1-2). The Psalms exemplify how a poor man shows his disposition by his prayer to Yahweh (Ps. 9-10; 25; 34; 37).

This religious conviction made Israel conscious of the manner in which Yahweh would ultimately bring about his salvation. The everlasting fidelity of Yahweh to his Covenant, the prophets say, chooses a so-called "Remnant," stripped of all earthly glamor, a better Israel, as the recipient of the promises of the New Covenant. The Messiah describes his mission as follows: "On that day you shall not be put to shame because of the deeds by which you have rebelled against me; for then I will remove from your midst your proudly exultant ones, and you shall no longer be haughty in my holy mountain. For I will leave in the midst of you a people humble and lowly. They shall seek refuge in the name of the Lord, those who are left in Israel; they shall do no wrong and utter no lies, nor shall there be found in their mouth a deceitful tongue. For they shall pasture and lie down, and none shall make them afraid" (Zeph. 3:11-13; cf. 2:3). And the Messiah describes his mission as follows: "The Spirit of the Lord God is upon me, because the Lord has anointed me to bring good tidings to the poor; he has sent me to bind up the brokenhearted, to proclaim liberty to the captives, and the opening of the prison to those who are bound; to proclaim the year of the Lord's favor, and the day of vengeance of our God" (Is. 61:1-2; cf. Is. 4:18-19).

Such Old Covenant spiritually reaches New Covenant fulfillment in the Sermon on the Mount. We read it in two versions; Matthew (5:3) says: "Blessed are the poor in spirit, for theirs is the kingdom of heaven"; according to Luke (6:20) the Lord says: "Blessed are you poor, for yours is the kingdom of God." In Matthew greater stress is put on the religious attitude of the heart ("poor in spirit"); his version seems to be more original. Luke evokes a broader Scriptural background: in the Old Testament we see a development of the concept "poor," namely, from a low social position to a really interior attitude of the heart, a consequence of this position. It is worthy of note that at the time of Christ the Jews in the community of Qumran again felt the need for a material foundation for the practice of their religious ideals. Entirely of their own free choice, the members of this confraternity, characterized by a spirit of "community" (cf. Acts 2:42; 2:44-45; 4:32, 34-35), adopted a way of life based on poverty. The evangelist, who often shows his preference for the poor, stresses this attitude as an ideal of Christian perfection, and confirms it by adding curses against the rich. This does not mean that Jesus, according to Luke, desired to canonize some aspect of social status; it does mean that, according to Jesus, some social situations dispose man to Christian perfection better than others.

This evaluation of poverty teaches us why Jesus himself chose poverty as a means of redemption. "Foxes have holes, and birds of the air have nests, but the Son of Man has nowhere to lay his head"

(Mt. 8:20; Lk. 9:58). The background from which
he says this is recognizable from the words which
follow immediately: "Another of the disciples said
to him: Lord, let me first go and bury my father.
But Jesus said to him: Follow me, and leave the
dead to bury their own dead" (Mt. 8:21-22; Lk.
9:59-60). His poverty is an expression of his desire
for complete self-effacement: "Come to me, all who
labor and are heavy laden, and I will give you
rest. Take my yoke upon you, and learn from me;
for I am gentle and lowly in heart, and you will find
rest for your souls. For my yoke is easy, and my
burden is light" (Mt. 11:28-30). His entry into
Jerusalem seated on a donkey was the fulfillment of
a prophecy of Zechariah (9:9); it signified the humble
and peaceful manner in which the Messiah was to
begin his reign (Mt. 21:1-11). The fact that in the
hour of his death he was deprived of his clothes
and had to endure mockery from his fellowmen was
used as proof of his messianic dignity (Mt. 27:35
and Jn. 19:24; cf. Ps. 22:19; Mt. 27:39-43; Ps. 22:8-9).
His self-affacement was the fulfillment of the proph-
ecies about the suffering Servant (cf. Is. 52:13; 53:12);
it was his obedience even unto death on the cross
(Phil. 2:6-8). Thus Christ himself, obedient to the
Father, accomplished redemption by means of poverty, suffering and failure, and ascribed a positive
value to real poverty in the Christian way of life.

The synoptics have composed a typical "handbook
of apostolic customs" (Mt. 10:5-14; Mk. 6:8-11; Lk.
9:1-5) in which, using a Palestinian literary genre,

they describe the ideal of poverty to be followed
by the apostles. Paul was inspired by the example
of the poor suffering Lord (2 Cor. 8:9; 4:1) when he
had to endure hardships (1 Cor. 4:11-12; 2 Cor.
11:9-27; 1:8-9; Phil. 4:11-14). We see in his life how
concrete circumstances forced him to invent new
means for practicing his ideal of poverty. Great
sums of money passed through his hands, — funds
for his livelihood (2 Cor. 11:8-9), collections for
Jerusalem, the compensation he offered to pay
Philemon for the damage caused by his runaway
slave (Philem. 1:19), the money which defrayed the
costs of sacrifices (Acts 21:23-24), the rent for his
house in Rome (Acts 28:30), the money which the
governor hoped to receive from him in prison (Acts
24:26).

Finally, perfect dedication to the Kingdom of God
acquires an added meaning by Jesus' demand that
those called to such a life, shall entirely renounce
all possessions (Mt. 19:21; Mk. 10:21; Lk. 18:22).
This poverty, freely assumed because of a special
divine vocation, is mentioned where Jesus uses as
an example the complete openness of the child (Mt.
19:13-15) and where, also from a Christian point of
view, he evaluates marriage and non-marriage (Mt.
19:10-12). Paul elaborates this still more extensively
from an eschatological position in his first letter to
the Corinthians when he speaks eloquently about
the nature of Christian marriage. When he introduces the topic of virginity, he also gives the motives
for a positive evaluation of freely accepted poverty:

"I mean, brethren, the appointed time has grown
very short; from now on, let those who have wives
live as though they had none, and those who mourn
as though they were not mourning, and those who
rejoice as though they were not rejoicing, and those
who buy as though they had no goods, and those
who deal with the world as though they had no deal-
ings with it. For the form of this world is passing
away" (1 Cor. 7:29-31). Thus freely accepted poverty, based on a divine vocation, is a sign that the
Church believes that the end time has arrived; this
sign is based on Christian hope.

CONCLUSION

We have attempted to show that the Bible knows
an asceticism which renounces the world. All practices of worldly renunciation which we meet in
other religions are found in the Scriptures. We
noted that as the religion of revelation takes on a
more interior and spiritualized form in a New Covenant, cultual asceticism gives way to religious asceticism.

Biblical asceticism which renounces the world is
distinguished from that of other religions because of
its inspired source. We never find pessimistic dualism in sacred writings (cf. chapter 1). There is
always consciousness of belief that we live in historical communion with the God of our salvation.
The various ascetic practices mentioned in the
course of the history of revelation take their origin
from a need to stress this awareness. Moreover, in

the New Covenant there is an entirely new and proper motive: the conviction that we live in the end time.

We need not deny that in Biblical asceticism we also see certain features of moral asceticism: an attempt to counterbalance the seduction of accepting the world by adopting a negative stance of rejecting it. Man because of his corporality is **in** the world and thus is readily inclined to live as if he were **of** the world. He always runs the risk of allowing the rhythm of his life to be determined by the rhythm of the cosmos. By doing so he belies what his faith teaches him — that the rhythm of his life must be determined by the historical reality of the God of his salvation in this world. Thus if the Bible takes to an asceticism of renouncing the world in following the ideal of the desert, this does not mean a complete rejection of sedentary culture. What it intends to point out is a way of life approaching as closely as possible the ideal of the Covenant: a community of life not based on the bonds of nature but on the bonds of loving free personal surrender. This is exactly why true asceticism, though it knows a renunciation of the world, is in last resort less "moral" or "cultual," than it is "mystical." This latter does not indicate a union with God acquired by man's own efforts; it is given to him by his sovereign God.

If we were to make an inventory of all ascetic practices of renouncing the world taught by the whole Bible it would result in a very meager list.

On the one hand, this would be the consequence of its fundamentally positive attitude toward the world. On the other hand, it might indicate that the Scriptures consider an ascetic **attitude** toward life more important than ascetic **practices**. Every man throughout his existence in this world must live in accord with an ascetic ideal inspired by the desert (cf. 1 Cor. 7:29-31); a Christian must live in the world but not be of the world. Ascetic practices are infrequently mentioned in the Bible. They serve only to confirm and emphasize an ascetic attitude. Special practices, accepting renunciation of the world as "a state of life" require a very special authorization from the sovereign historical God of salvation, a special vocation (cf. Mt. 19:21; Mk. 10:21; Lk. 18:22).

Finally there remains one question: what moves the God of salvation, who also is the God of creation, to establish a relativity of value regarding this material world? We grant that he has the right to do this. But certainly if he makes the value of our material world relative, he will not do this whimsically, without a motive we are able to understand. We will speak about this in our next chapter.

3

GOD'S HEALING LOVE

Biblical asceticism is basically determined by the historical character of salvation and consequently is a positive attitude toward the world (cf. above, chapter 1). The spirituality of the desert (cf. chapter 2), as found in the Bible, is not a departure from the world, but is an emphasis on the historical character of salvation as taught by revelation. Faith however in an "end time," suggesting that the form of this world passes away (cf. chapter 1), shows that our positive attitude toward the world can only be a relative one. This relativity must also affect the nature of Biblical asceticism. What this means depends entirely on the answer to the question: Whence this relativity of our positive attitude toward the world because of our faith in an end time?

This question brings us to the problem of evil in this world. In its struggle against infection by the local religion of sedentary Canaan, Israel more and more acquired the religious conviction that salvation could come only from the God of history. He so arranged things that sedentary Israel had to renounce all hope of receiving salvation from ritual observances performed according to Canaanite myths.

Israel's salvation lay in its own history and it was impossible to obtain it outside of that history.

Nevertheless, this struggle against the seductions of the local cult was Israel's severest trial; more than by anything else it was purified by it. During this time the chosen people was most emphatically confronted with the problem of evil in man's existence in the world, because this was the time when it had to endure the heaviest calamities. Faith here came into overt contradiction with immediate experience. According to our experience, is not temporariness a synonym for subjection to evil and corruption? How then can history be salvific according to faith?

The Bible must take the standpoint that temporality does not necessarily include evil and corruption for man. It can be an instrument of salvation as well as a factor of corruption. The big question is how faith and experience are related to one another.

1. Ancient man without revelation

Even outside the Bible man did not always adopt an exclusively pessimistic outlook on the temporality of human existence. The uniqueness of the Biblical religious point of view becomes more evident if we acquaint ourselves with the opinions the Semitic and Greek world, the milieu in which revelation originated and operated. It will also become more evident that this revelation was an enormous contribution for man in his efforts to find an answer to the tantalizing problem of evil.

(a) **The ancient Semites.** Ancient man had en-

during memories of a catastrophic event, immemo-
rially long ago, which was the starting point of the
decadence of the material world. Originally, they
thought that when the gods and the universe came
into being, heaven and earth were interconnected.
Old Babylonian temple towers (of which the Bible's
tower of Babel is a remembrance) seem to point to
this fact. Thus the temple tower of Larsa was
called "the house of the bond between heaven and
earth," the one of Babel "house of the foundation
of heaven and earth," the one of Borsippa "house of
the seven leaders of heaven and earth." It seems
the people in this way expressed a human attempt
to restore lost contact with the deity. A legend
akin to this holds that there is, in the far East,
a center of the world where, according to a certain
version of the Mesopotamian epos of Gilgamesh,
the hero of the story is looking for the herb of life.
He finds it in the depth of the primeval ocean
after meeting the Babylonian Noah, who escaped
from the great Flood and leads an immortal life on
the isle of the blessed.

This unique moment, when heaven and earth
and time and eternity still were one, was the time
of paradisic unity between gods and man (cf. Gen.
2-3). In this communion the movements of the entire
cosmos and all possible manifestations of human
culture were determined in their ideal form; this
was to be the norm and the source of all events in
the world. One fatal fault spoiled this original
paradisic solidarity and destroyed the harmony exist-

ing between the time of the gods and the time of
nature. Henceforth man was to stand between these
two times. The time of nature leads to death,
though it has not lost its character as a manifestation
of divine powers.

This Babylonian tradition has some similarity with
our doctrine of original sin. In the Adapa myth we
are told how the Babylonian Adam, through the
(misleading?) interference of a god, failed to lay
hold of the gift of immortality offered him. From
this moment connection between heaven and earth,
between time and eternity was broken; man receded
further and further from his original paradisic condition and was doomed to eventually die. Once he
died there was no hope whatsoever of a life in the
hereafter. His body, made of loam, returns to the
earth from which it is taken, and his spirit descends
into the underworld, from which no return is possible.

Yet paradise is not entirely lost. In the phenomena
of life in nature and of the human community a
creative order manifests itself spontaneously and
continuously; this is a vestige of the beneficent
reality of the world of gods from which man in the
beginning had broken away. Life in the universe
works itself out according to the archetypes of the
ideal original time and nourishes itself from them.
The cosmic time of nature with its rhythm of day
and night, or ascent and descent, of life and death
might be called a sacrament of eternity. In its
unceasing repetition of ever-identically ascending

and descending waves it is a return to the original condition of things. Death is thus a return to the original chaotic ocean, in which there is a vague expectancy of resurrection and new life.

This little remnant of lost paradise kept alive in man the hope that he might again lay hold of his lost happiness. Therefore when the change from death to new life took place in nature, ancient Babylon celebrated the feast of New Year. This was depicted as a struggle between the old and the new year; it would remain unresolved if the rite did not bring about the triumph of the new year. For twelve days the mythological drama of the enthronement of the god Marduk was ritually enacted. The central cultual text was an epos of creation describing the mythological primeval struggle between order and disorder, world and chaos, light and darkness, life and death, the gods and the hostile powers. In it the gods deplore the fate of Marduk, who is kept a prisoner in the underworld by the powers of death. Led by Marduk's son Nabu they liberated the captive deity. The ruling king of Babylon usually played the role of Marduk in these liturgical scenes.

When Marduk (the king) had been liberated from the chaotic powers of death he was led in a triumphal procession to the festive building outside the city where the celebration continued. On the second last day they returned to the city where Marduk (the king) made his triumphal entry and again took his place on the throne, ruling now over a purified city and a renewed world.

By celebrating the Babylonian feast of New Year in this way man tried to escape his fatal situation by ritualizing his time. By this stylized imitation of the paradisic archetype he tried as far as possible to rule out his own time, which leads to death; by acting out this privileged ritual moment he tried to taste, in retrospect, something of the paradisic completeness. These celebrations unmistakably must be considered destructive to the human person: what is inevitable in man is really displaced here.

We are forced to conclude that this Babylonian answer to the problem of evil is a consequence of its ahistorical concept of time. This becomes more evident when we compare it with the Biblical view. Holy Scripture is interested only in the historical God of salvation and speaks about "a beginning" of creation (cf. Gen. 1:1); historical time has its inception with this beginning. God's existence "before" creation is of a quite different order; it cannot be experienced and cannot be expressed in words. It lies outside the perspective of the Bible, which looks only at the historical relationship between God and the created world. This relation is the union of the God of the Covenant with his people. This simultaneously implies recognition of God's transcendence and of his immanence, of God's existence above time and his historical reality in time.

The myth presumes a period before and after

creation. Before creation is the time of the deity's coming into being and of his struggle with the chaotic powers. From the myth of creation acted out on the feast of New Year, it is evident how important the role of this dramatic period of the creator-god is for the act of creation itself: it is the personal drama of the deity himself, who by his victory over chaos creates order, the cosmos. But these vanquished powers still frequently rebel against their "creator." The Adapa myth tells of the deity Ea, a traitor among the gods, who incites the Babylonian Adam, Adapa, to refuse the bread and the potion of life offered him by the god Anu. Ever since that moment man is doomed to die. Thus in the mythical view there would seem to be no distinction between the time before creation and after it.

We must here recognize an unmistakable, though not explicitly mentioned, dualism: the existence of the powers of darkness and light, of chaos and cosmos, of death and life in constant conflict. No wonder man realized his helplessness when confronted with relentless cosmic time which led him to death. So he threw himself into the intoxications of the orgy (cf. the agrarian rites of Canaan); this allowed him to forget his fatal situation. Nature here is no longer a sign of God's benignity to man. It is the embodiment of an impersonal chaotic power, by which man allows himself to be swallowed. For the mythical mind, the problem of evil remained an unsolvable mystery.

(b)   In the **Greek world**[11] the problem of evil was
explicitly treated only by Plato. Socrates was still
so impressed by the order in the universe and the
efficiency of nature that he firmly believed in a
wise providence directing everything for the good
of man. Even to the judges who had condemned
him to death he says: "You also, judges, must keep
good hope as to death. You should keep well in mind
this indubitable truth: For a good man there is
no evil, neither after his death nor during his life,
and his fate is not neglected by the gods. What is
happening now to me is not a thing that just happens
incidentally. To me it is evident that it is better
for me to be dead and liberated from difficulties"
(Plato, Apol. 41 c^8 — e^1).

Even in his later works Plato was convinced that
only good things come from God, though evil is
stronger in this world. He so admired cosmic harmony that he saw in it a proof of the existence of
God. The considerable moral evil in the world he
ascribes to man's own fault. The cause of physical
evil is not exclusively due to the materiality of the
world; nevertheless, we find here an explanation
for the possibility of this evil matter which by
nature is necessarily limited. Since the cosmos is
sometimes left to itself by the ruler of the universe,
it must look after itself as well as possible, relying
on its remembrance of the lessons of its father, the
demiurge. Here, because of the nature of matter,
things may sometimes go awry. Divine providence
however has ordered everything in such a way that

evil in the cosmos can easily be overcome by good. It is man's task to bring this about, and in doing so he may expect the help of the gods.

For his concept of time, Plato begins from the cycle of all movement. He held that the rhythm of the cosmos is determined by an endless repetition of coming up and going down, of life and death, of renewal and decay. This cyclic view of time however does not seduce him to any pessimism as regards man's final destiny. God's goodness is a guarantee that man never need despair of his salvation.

The Stoics reached a conclusion which would have been inconceivable to Plato's religious mind. Adopting the idea of a cycle of all events in this world, and depressed by this fatalistic situation, they did not hesitate to accuse God: they felt that divine providence is sorely in need of rational justification regarding the problem of evil. This is therefore the chief tenet of their doctrine about God. They explain evil by the restrictions material beings impose on divine providence; or by the fact that individual suffering is subservient to the maintenance of the whole; or, because everything necessarily has a reverse side (which of course is not true), good also has one; or, because God uses suffering as a peda- gogical means (just as the best athletes become superior by the most severe training) so also man must consider it an honor if God strikes him so heavily that he becomes immune to all suffering. There is a great contrast between this bow to pride and the Biblical ideal of humility as a consequence of trials suffered (cf. the figure of Job). Typically, the Stoics place the solution of the problem of evil entirely in their concept of fate. There is a wide difference between such a viewpoint and that of Plato who exhorted man to endure the tension between a positive attitude to the world and an attitude of renouncing it.

According to the gnostic religious mentality which dominated the hellenist world at the beginning of our era, this visible world is not evidence of a watchful divine providence. Matter is bad because of a mythological event, either through man's own fault or through the fault of one of the lower beings which — escaping from a more or less impersonal transcendent deity — committed the crime of creating a material world. Practically, they think only in terms of duality: matter and spirit, darkness and light, time and eternity, good and evil. Temporality is not much more than a caricature of eternity — an illusion in which man's personal freedom is crippled, all historical inevitability is denied. Here there is room only for a radical renunciation of the world and consequently man tries as best he possibly can to wrest himself from evil matter in order to unite himself with the unknown God by a knowledge which makes him profess his eternal origin.

2. The starting point of Biblical religious reflection

In the Bible we meet a world of thought entirely different from any other religion. This is true because of its monotheistic concept of God which cannot conceive of a deity wrestling with chaos and other powers. It is likewise true because of the historical reality of the Scriptures' God, who enters into a personal relationship with man. The salutary fact of God as creator allows for full development of free will in the human person. Deep conviction that the saving God is the all-powerful being was the reason why the problem of evil in the Old Covenant was explicitly treated only rather late in history.

Near the mountain of Sinai, the Covenant was entered into between Yahweh and the small Israelitic community. At that time Israel had not yet acquired a formal awareness of the monotheistic character of its God (as we find in Is. 40-55 and Gen. 1). In the Ten Commandments Yahweh declares himself to be the national God who does not allow any rival gods, "for I the Lord your God am a jealous God, visiting the iniquity of the fathers upon the children to the third and the fourth generation of those who hate me, but showing steadfast love to thousands of those who love me and keep my commandments" (Ex. 20:5). From this text it is evident that Israel now knows quite well where evil comes from: it is a necessary consequence of not measuring up to the Covenant. The chosen people know that their God is much more inclined to beneficence than to punishment (cf. the contrast between "third .and fourth generation" and the "thousandth generation"). This idea, that parents are punished in their offspring, shows that the Israelites had a very strong feeling of solidarity. Moreover, their concept of retribution does not seem to go beyond the earthly horizon.

Israel inherited these ideas from its forefathers. It is said that the patriarchs were "gathered to their people" (Gen. 25:8; 35:39; 49:33; cf. 25:17), or went to "lie with their fathers" (Gen. 47:30). They probably thought that the deceased lived in the grave together with his forefathers — an idea we meet also in ancient Egypt, in Babylon and Canaan, where people gave food to their dead and regularly supplied them with water. This strong community feeling is characteristic of nomadic life, where the struggle for life closely binds the members of a family or a clan together.

Although death was considered a fatal event for man, it was not looked upon as something which made the meaning of human existence a problem. Israel knew there is a time of coming and a time of going for everything. Thus Joshua in his farewell speech to the leaders of the people says: "And now I am about to go the way of all the earth" (Jos. 23:14). Death is a normal and natural phenomenon in the existence of man, because he is part of this perishable material world. As long as Yahweh's saving reality was placed explicitly within earthly boundaries, the highest ideal could be only to die "in a good old age" (Judg. 8:32; cf. Gen. 25:8; 35:29).

This does not mean that they had no belief whatsoever in man's real survival after death. From early times, the graves of great people were a center of veneration. In later times too the graves of Abraham and Sarah were shown in the grotto of Macpelah (Gen. 23:19; 25:9). According to the

Yahwist tradition there is a grave of Jacob (Gen.
50:5; 47:30), possibly on a piece of land which he
himself bought in Sichem (Gen. 33:19), where his
son Joseph was later buried (Jos. 24:32). Further,
there are still graves of Deborah (Gen. 35:8), of
Rebekah's nurse (35:8), of Rachel (Gen. 35:19 ff.),
of Joshua (Jos. 24:30) and many others. It seems
probable that the meetings under the old oak at
Sichem (Jos. 24; 1 Kings 12) were close to the
grave of Joseph (and Jacob). Egypt and Greece
held strong convictions on survival of the dead; in
Canaan, on the contrary, the painful experience of
departure from earthly life was especially emphasized. Death here was not considered an apotheosis,
but the sad end of man's life, as is evident from the
dirges accompaning the descent into the **sheol,** the
underworld (Gen. 37:33 ff.; 2 Sam. 1:19-27 — dying
is falling).

Israel's original view of the sheol, confirms this.
Every mortal is doomed to go there. It is situated
deep under the ground with an entrance at the
bottom of the primeval sea; it is dark and dusty.
Absolute silence reigns, because there is no activity
whatsoever — no religious activity either, such as
singing God's praises. The existence of the deceased
is reduced to an extreme minimum. They were
sometimes called "the weak ones," because all vital
force had ebbed from them; God had taken back
the spirit of life he once had given them. Sheol is
a place of forgetting and being forgotten, it seems,
even by Yahweh. No return is ever possible.[12]

It is quite understandable that death was a real horror for the religious Israelite. Reaching a very old age, as tangible proof of God's lasting favor, alone could assuage its gloom. To be taken from the earthly community of the living, the object of Yahweh's interest and kindness, was equivalent to banishment from God's view. A good or bad life on earth made no difference at all in the hereafter. Here we clearly see the influence of the strong feeling of community of which we have spoken.

This concept is also why the meaning of human existence did not become a problem for the individual Israelite if he had to suffer innocently. The blessings of the national redeeming God were the only ones given in this material world: physical welfare or adversity depended on the moral behavior of the Israelitic community, their fidelity or infidelity to the God of the Covenant.

Evidently, from the very beginning of revelation Israel was well aware of the fact that evil plays an important role in the world. For this they needed no explanation based on fate. When Yahweh punished them for their sins by physical calamities, they knew that this was not God's ultimate answer: their faith in him as a national saving God remained unshaken, and they were able to see God's punishing verdict as a grace.

We may recall here a Scriptural view mentioned in our first chapter: in spite of the fact that they expected material rewards for their fidelity to Yah-

weh, they still thought that being united to him
was the supreme blessing. Since entering into the
underworld meant the end of all union with God
for the Israelite, life and death from the beginning
were ideas which had not only a physical but a
religious meaning as well: obedience to God brings
life, sin saps life and leads to death.

3. The prophets

Israel had no problem with the meaning of human
life. Though death was considered tragic, the people
had abundant opportunities to enjoy Yahweh's blessings in this earthly life.

Along the difficult road of its calamitous history
however Israel gradually became aware of the fact
that Yahwism still contained an unexepected treasure.
Never in the history of the Old Covenant was the
sinfulness of Israel and of all mankind so realistic-
ally described, nor was the inexhaustible and limitless saving love of Yahweh for Israel and the world
put into such moving words as was done in the
period of the prophets.

We can describe, in a somewhat schematic way,
the different stages of the evolution of this consciousness:

(a) The prophets' condemnations are directed
mostly against Israel's infidelity to the Covenant in
the time of the kings.

The school of "older prophets" describes all Israel,
north as well as south, as a sinful and therefore a
rejected people. A slight reservation however is

made, which will later prove to be of very great importance.

The verdict on the northern kingdom was absolutely negative: all the kings did "what was evil in the sight of the Lord" — like Jeroboam (1 Kings 15:26, 34 etc.), even Zimri, who reigned only for seven days (16:19), or Jehu, the strict Yahwist (2 Kings 10:29-32). This kingdom definitely came to an end with the fall of Samaria (722; 2 Kings 17:15). The author describes the motives of this punishment of Yahweh in detail: they "had feared other gods and walked in the customs of the nations whom the Lord drove out before the people of Israel" (2 Kings 17:7-8; cf. the whole pericope, verses 7-18).

"None was left but the tribe of Judah (the southern kingdom) only" (2 Kings 17:18), as the only heir of the Yahwist blessings. "Judah also did not keep the commandments of the Lord their God, but walked in the customs which Israel (the northern kingdom) had introduced. And the Lord rejected all the descendants of Israel, and afflicted them, and gave them into the hand of spoilers, until he had cast them out of his sight" (2 Kings 17:19-20). The kingdom of Judah remained for 135 years. The last chapter of 2 Kings (25) describes its sad end. Of its last king, Zedekiah, we read (2 Kings 24:19-20): "And he did what was evil in the sight of the Lord, according to all that Jeroboam had done. For because of the anger of the Lord it came to the point in Jerusalem and Judah that he cast them out from his presence."

The "later (writing) prophets" threatened Israel with the "Day of Yahweh" because of its national infidelity. The prophets always speak about this day as about something generally known to the people. But before the exile we note that there was a strong need to correct the people's mistaken opinion that this was "a day to be desired" (cf. Amos 5:18). It had to be presented as a threat for a sinful people. "The day of the Lord . . . it is darkness, and not light, and gloom with no brightness in it . . . I will take you into exile beyond Damascus," says Yahweh, when he threatens the northern kingdom with the Assyrian exile through the lips of the Judean farmer, Amos (cf. 8:9-10; 2:16).

But Judah must also know, Isaiah says, "that the day of the Lord comes" to break their pride, and to make their gods disappear into the holes and caves of the earth out of fear for the Lord and for the splendor of his glory; then they will learn to "turn away from man in whose nostrils is breath, for of what account is he?" (Is. 2:6-22). According to Jeremiah (30:5-7) that day is more terrifying than any other. According to Zephaniah (1:15; cf. 1:4-18): "A day of wrath is that day, a day of distress and anguish, a day of ruin and devastation, a day of darkness and gloom, a day of clouds and thick darkness." "None escaped or survived; those whom I handled and reared my enemy destroyed." Jerusalem later wails, when her children have disappeared and she herself is left in ruins (Lam. 2:22).

In this stage, Israel still envisages the problem of

evil only on a national level. It is restricted to their
own earthly reality.

(b) Beside the sinfulness of their own nation the
prophets also spoke about the sinfulness of others
(cf. Amos 1:2-3; Is. 30:27-33; 31; Mic. 5:14; Zeph.
2:4-15; Jer. 9:24-25 etc.). They did not as yet draw
the same conclusions for the pagans as they did
for the Jews (Deut. 2:14; Jer. 5:1; 6:14; 16:11-12
etc.), namely, that they were sinful from their
ancestors on (cf. the "national hereditary sin" in Ex.
32).

The idea of some sort of hereditary sinfulness of
the entire human race is the unique revelation of
the Yahwist tradition in the story of paradise (Gen.
2-3). But even there the belief that the children
share in the sinfulness and punishment of the ances-
tor — as found in most of the prophets in their
principle of solidarity — is still prevalent. That the
first sin had its interior consequences for the whole
human race — a thought which in a way was only
implicitly uttered in Gen. 2-3 — was not explicitly
mentioned until later by Paul in his letter to the
Romans. Each man shares from his birth — prior to
any personal decision of his own — in a general
situation of estrangement, namely, in the loss of the
supernatural community of grace and in the impos-
sibility of being entirely good (cf. Rom. 5:6 ff.). The
reign of death and sin however, which began with
Adam's sin, comes to full reality only through the
personal sin of his descendants.[13]

A new element in the story of Gen. 2-3 is that punishment for sin is not restricted to the unhappy lot of man upon earth, but even death is punishment. A consequence of the sin of paradise is that man falls back to the condition which was his by nature — he is mortal: "In the sweat of your face you shall eat bread till you return to the ground, for out of it you were taken; and to dust you shall return" (Gen. 3:19; cf. 2:7).

Israel's awareness that Yahweh rules over the whole world helps answer the question of the origin of evil. In the course of their history their faith has shown them that Yahweh is a "living God" (Deut. 5:26; Jos. 3:10; 1 Sam. 17:26; 2 Kings 19:4) and that as such he is different from all pagan gods (Jer. 10:8 ff.; Is. 44:9-20). That he is also a saving God is fully manifested only when he makes man live. Hence the gift of the "tree of life" (Gen. 2:9; 3:22, 24), which enabled man to "live for ever" (Gen. 3:22).

Concretely, man's situation (Gen. 3:16-19) is one of calamity, for which he alone, not God, is responsible. Sin is an action which breaks community with the living God and necessarily brings death (also for the body — going away into the underworld, the territory forgotten by the living God). One fact is expressed in various ways: with the increase of moral evil man also loses his physical strength. According to the Yahwist tradition the maximum age of man is restricted to 120 years (Gen. 6:3), because of the commingling of the sons of God with the daughters of men. The priestly tradition also speaks about a gradual decrease of the span of human life: from Adam to Noah 900 - 700 years (Gen. 5), from Shem to Terah 500 - 200 years (Gen. 11:10-32), from Abraham to Jacob 200 - 100 years (Gen. 25:7, 17; 35:28; 47:9). In this way Genesis gives an explanation of physical evil in this world: it is not due to fate, it is not inherent to the temporality of human existence, but is the result of man's revolt against God.

(c) Whatever happens to Israel — both the northern and the southern kingdom may be exiled — faith in Yahweh as the God of salvation must not be forsaken. Was this not the prophecy of Nathan to David, in which Yahweh assures his servant: "Your house and your kingdom shall be made sure for ever before me, your throne shall be established for ever" (2 Sam. 7:16; cf. verses 4:16)? Moses had already alluded to the future destiny of the chosen people; he had pointed out that where Yahweh is there is always hope: "But from there you will seek the Lord your God, and you will find him, if you search after him with all your heart and with all your soul. When you are in tribulation, and all these things come upon you in the latter days, you will return to the Lord your God and obey his voice, for the Lord your God is a merciful God; he will not fail you or destroy you or forget the covenant with your fathers which he swore to them" (Deut. 4:29-31; cf. verses 25-31). The prayer of Solomon during the dedication of the temple testified to his unswerving confidence in the saving God; he maintained this even when the chosen people, Yahweh's inheritance, is led away into exile. If, repenting, they ask him for his help he will give it (1 Kings 8:46-53). The author of the book of the Kings did not have a single good word to say about the kings of the northern kingdom, where one dynasty succeeded the other; but in his judgment of the kings of Judah he varies his evaluation of them from good, relatively good, to very good. Although Manasseh is described in the Bible as the paragon of sinfulness and is punished by exile in Assyria (2 Kings 21:1; 18; cf. 2 Chron. 33:1-20), the author acknowledges that in the southern kingdom Yahweh remained faithful to the Davidic dynasty up to the time of the exile. He concludes by saying: "And in the thirty-seventh year of the exile of Jehoiachin king of Judah, in the twelfth month, on the twenty-seventh day of the month, Evil-merodach king of Babylon, in the year that he began to reign, graciously freed Jehoiachin king of Judah from prison; and he spoke kindly to him, and gave him a seat above the seats of the kings who were with him in Babylon. So Jehoiachin put off his prison garments. And every day of his life he dined regularly at the king's table; and a regular allowance was given him by the king, every day a portion, as long as he lived" (2 Kings 25:27-30). Is not this privilege which befalls Jehoiachin at the court of Babel a sign that Yahweh is engaged once more in taking up the threads of the history of salvation? Jehoiachin is twice called "the king of Judah" whose seat was "above the seats of the kings who were with him in Babylon." It looks like a profession of faith of the author in Yahweh's unswerving fidelity to the dynasty of Jesse's son.

Substantially, this is the only thing the prophets continue to announce. For this reason their appeal is so passionate. Unable to forget the love with which he has surrounded Israel from the beginning of its existence, Yahweh exclaims: "My heart recoils within me, my compassion grows warm and tender. I will not execute my fierce anger, I will not again destroy Ephraim; for I am God and not man, the Holy One in your midst, and I will not come to destroy" (Hos. 11:8-9). Yahweh's love for the ancestors, which made him choose them among all the peoples of the earth (Deut. 10:15; cf. 4:37; 7:8) is "an everlasting love" (Jer. 31:3). Yahweh will insistently try to gain his bride again, to give her the joy she had in the days when she came out of Egypt (Hos. 2:8-17). There will be a new betrothal, but now it will last for ever (Hos. 2:21-24; Zeph. 3:17). "In overflowing wrath for a moment I hid my face from you, but with everlasting love I will have compassion on you, says the Lord, your Redeemer" (Is. 54:8). "Because you are precious in my eyes, and honored, and I love you, I give men in return for you, peoples in exchange for your life. Fear not, for I am with you . . ." (Is. 43:4 ff.). "Can a woman forget her sucking child, that she should have no compassion on the son of her womb? Even these may forget, yet I will not forget you. Behold, I have graven you on the palms of my hands; your walls are continually before me" (Is. 49:14-16).

The failure of the Old Covenant — both the northern and the southern kingdoms were in exile — and their continuing faith in Yahweh as the God of salvation are the reasons which make them yearn for a New Covenant in which God's initiative will be more active. "I will put my law within them, and I will write it upon their hearts . . . and no longer shall each man teach his neighbor . . . saying: Know Lord, for they shall all know me, from the least of them to the greatest . . ." (cf. Jer. 31:31-34). At the same time they develop an awareness of the positive significance of human suffering in the world: it is a punishment caused by human sin; but it is also a judgment of God by which he purifies and selects. God will sift with a seive unfaithful Israel from among all peoples (Amos 9:8-10) till only a "Remnant" is left (cf. Is. 6:13; Mic. 5:2). "The remnant of the trees of his forest will be so few that a child can write them down. In that day the remnant of Israel and the survivors of the house of Jacob will no more lean upon him that smote them, but will lean upon the Lord, the Holy One of Israel, in truth. A remnant will return, the remnant of Jacob, to the mighty God" (Is. 10:19-21; cf. Is. 7:3; Jer. 3:14; 5:18; Ezek. 5:3; 9, etc.). "For I will leave in the midst of you a people humble and lowly. They shall seek refuge in the name of the Lord" (Zeph. 3:12). "The lame I will make the remnant, and those who were cast off, a strong nation and the Lord will reign over them in Mount Zion from this time forth and for evermore" (Mic. 4:7; cf. Is. 4:2-3; 28:5-6; 37:31-32; Zeph. 2:7-9).

This idea of a remnant develops through the
centuries. In the beginning, it includes those who
are left after the punishment of sinful Israel and
are converted to Yahweh. Requital still is on the
national level and of an earthly nature: restoration
of Jerusalem and of the Davidic dynasty. Gradually
the word takes on a religious meaning: "those who
are entirely open to God" (cf. above Zeph. 3:12, and
chapter 2, "the poor"). The requital now is much
more universal and spiritual.

The formula of the New Covenant, according to
Jeremiah (31:31-34), shows the old ideas of collective
requital abandoned and a higher idea, the personal
value of the individual acknowledged. Ezekiel argues
for individual responsibility. He considered his experience with Jerusalem (Ezek. 8-10) proof that
Yahweh rewards or punishes every one according
to his actual (not even his former) personal attitude
(14:12-21; cf. 18; 3:16b-21; 33:1-20). While Ezekiel
claims individual requital immediately, a later addi-
tion to the prophetic works of Jeremiah (31:29-30),
places this in the future. Ezekiel and Jeremiah,
although broad in their perspective, remained within
the horizon of this material world.

(d) An entirely new aspect of the positive value
of human suffering is poignantly expressed in the
poems about the mysterious "Servant of Yahweh."
Toward the end of the Babylonian captivity an
anonymous author sings about the union between
God and man, broken through sin, to be restored in
the messianic time. Because of the sins of many

people, a mysterious figure, later identified with
the New Testament Christ — the "Suffering Servant"
— though innocent, is put to death. Suffering of the
innocent had already been mentioned by Jeremiah
(5:1) and Ezekiel (22:30) who pointed out that God
would forgive Jerusalem if he would find only one
just man (cf. Gen. 18). In the fourth song (Is. 52:13;
53:12) the innocent personal suffering of the Servant
is rewarded by Yahweh with long life beyond the
grave, and a numerous posterity is to share this
with him. The later Isaiah tradition therefore looks
for a new heaven and a new earth, where man's
life span will again be as it was before the fall (Is.
65:17-25).

The extreme individualism of Ezekiel is cor-
rected in these songs by the belief that personal
suffering can accomplish much for the redemption of
the human community. Here there is no commercial
haggling with God to buy off something. Here we
find the belief that God acknowledges the value of
a person, if this person, puts himself entirely at the
disposal of his sovereign will for the redemption of
mankind. Here we have the Old Testament summit
of the traditional faith in Yahweh's absolute will
that every one shall be saved.

As to the meaning of human suffering, there is
a certain parallelism with another theme mentioned
in the Old Testament: the theme of the "Remnant,"
of which we have spoken. There too we find the
idea that Yahweh's saving activity will reach its
full development in the re-creation of a new people

of God in a New Covenant. This will take place in the "dispersed among the gentiles" (Bar. 2:13; Ezek. 6:8-9; Deut. 30:1-2; Jer. 23:3), "the crippled" (Mic. 4:7), "the humble and lowly" (Zeph. 3:12) who "broken of heart" (cf. Deut. 30:1-2; Ezek. 6:9-10) "call upon the name of the Lord" (Joel 3:5; Zech. 13:8-9); the fulfillment of all will be the Christ, the "shoot of the stump of Jesse" (Is. 11:1, 10). The theme of the remnant points to the divine process of the sorting out, in the first place of the people of God; after this, other remnants, even individuals, will be included: this is a process of sifting which for the individual person takes the form of purification to the very marrow of his being. This activity of the saving God continues until in the end it reaches the suffering servant, Jesus Christ, who is entirely dedicated to him and "by whose stripes we are healed" (Is. 53:5; 1 Pet. 2:24). Here we have the moment in which the consequences of sin, suffering and death become salutary for man because of God's merciful love.

The theme of poverty (cf. above, chapter 2) thus acquires its deepest dimension.

4. After the exile

The time of vigorous prophetic inspiration ends when the crisis it was to overcome ends. Henceforth Israel lives on its glorious past. The only question which occupies the minds in this period concerns the requital and the meaning of evil. The prophets had already ascribed a positive meaning to evil (cf. above 3.c and 3.d). They had exploded the

principle of collective requital and its earthly horizon. But these solutions were too vague to be
satisfactory.

Early parts of the book of Proverbs (after the
exile) still give an old fashioned solution, and the
author maintains that experience confirms it: the
good are rewarded and the evil are punished in this
life (3:33-35; 9:6-18). The book of Job (5th century
B.C.) shows its doubt of this in a dramatic way.
The three friends uselessly defend the traditional
view of a requital within this world, and the author
cannot find any other solution but entrusting himself, in spite of all, in faith to God and to bow
resigned before his mystery. It is sufficient to be
united with the mysterious God. The book of Eccle-
siastes (beginning of the 2nd century), though speaking in an entirely different tone, gives the same
solution: this author also dwells on the insufficiency
(vanity, absurdity) of the usual answers. He rejects the opinion that man can demand a reckoning
from God and that he is entitled to claim happiness
as a right. He has an inkling of the doctrine of the
"last times," but he expresses it indistinctly. He
merely comes to the conclusion that life in any case
is better than death.

We find a clearly sufficient answer only in Daniel
(12:1 ff.; cf. 2 Macc. 7:9, 14 — 124 B.C.), though this
is restricted to the collectivity. Since life after death,
about which he speaks, is explicitly described as
eternal, it necessarily postulates bodily resurrection.
For the Semite, death does not mean that a subsist-

ent principle of life leaves the confines of the body. It means a debilitation, an ebbing away of all vitality in a living being. This religious conclusion was the result of a consequent development of several revealed truths: Yahweh's limitless power over the underworld, the belief that God will requite justly, the Yahwist expectation of salvation for the chosen people; because of these Ezekiel was able to speak of a national resurrection from the graveyard of exile (37:1-4).

From hellenistic sources, such as Alexandria, the ancient faith received new ways of thought (considering the immortal soul as a principle of life) which strengthened its belief in survival after death. The Hebrew, unlike a Westerner, had no concept of man being composed of body and soul; this was developed under the influence of hellenistic thought. "Soul" meant man as a living being; "flesh" meant man as a bodily being. We find some traces of the new forms of thought in the book of Wisdom (written by an Alexandrian Jew in the 1st century B.C.). He holds that suffering in this world does not serve for the purpose of conversion, penance, satisfaction and reconciliation. He considers it a necessary part of divine pedagogy, (testing our fidelity, safeguarding us against the seduction of evil, showing God's benignity) which leads the faithful to eternal life with God in the hereafter. Though bodily resurrection is not explicitly mentioned in this book, it seems presumed: immortality is imperishable life, which through bodily resurrection will be the lot of the elect (cf. 6:18 ff.; 3:4; 1:15). This belief in a

bodily resurrection answered a long-felt need in
Israel: man should not only be appreciated as an
individual human person, but should also be acknowledged as a fellowman.

5. The New Covenant

In his letter to the Romans Paul describes the
human situation as the history of man's perdition.
But this was not the main point he wanted to
teach. What he wished to stress above all is the
unlimited energy with which God's constant fidelity
decisively reconciled the world to himself through
Christ, thus restoring the community of love in him
(cf. 5:5), not for a time but for ever. "But the free
gift is not like the trespass. For if man died through
one man's trespass, much more have the grace of
God and the free gift in the grace of that one man
Jesus Christ abounded for many. And the free gift
is not like the effect of that one man's sin. For
the judgment following one trespass brought condemnation, but the free gift following many tres-
passes brings justification. If, because of one man's
trespass, death reigned through that one man, much
more will those who receive the abundance of grace
and the free gift of righteousness reign in life
through the one man Jesus Christ. Then as one
man's trespass led to condemnation for all men, so
one man's act of righteousness leads to acquittal
and life for all men. For as by one man's disobedience
many were made sinners, so by one man's obedience
many will be made righteous. Law came in, to
increase the trespass; but where sin increased, grace

abounded all the more, so that, as sin reigned in death, grace also might reign through righteousness to eternal life through Jesus Christ our Lord" (Rom. 5:15-21).

In Jesus Christ is accomplished whatever God in the Old Testament — especially in the prophecy of the suffering servant — taught man to desire: human existence now is extremely meaningful, even though — or perhaps especially because — it must bear innumerable afflictions in this world. Suffering and death are a punishment for all who enter human existence and as such start on the road to irrevocable and total destruction. The fact however that the living God, out of merciful love, deigned to share this existence with us in the man Jesus Christ, has made the destructive forces of suffering and death into a healing force unto eternal life.

In speaking to the inhabitants of Philippi, Paul also says to us: "Have this mind among yourselves, which you have in Christ Jesus, who, though he was in the form of God, did not count equality with God a thing to be grasped, but emptied himself, taking the form of a servant, being born in the likeness of men. And being found in human form, he humbled himself and became obedient unto death even death on a cross. Therefore God has highly exalted him and bestowed on him the name which is above every name, that at the name of Jesus every knee should bow, in heaven and on earth and under the earth, and every tongue confess that Jesus Christ is Lord, to the glory of God the Father" (2:5-11).

A dying Christian may feel himself entirely forsaken by God, as happened to Christ on the cross (cf. Mt. 27:46 and par.; but if he has acquired an attitude of self-denying love and accepts this abandonment, it becomes for him and for his fellowmen the road to eternal life,[15] because of his mystical union with the dead and risen Lord (cf. Rom. 6:4 ff.).

CONCLUSION

After thus devoutly reading the Bible it becomes evident to us that Biblical asceticism is not concerned with a positive or negative attitude toward the material world, but with the acceptance of God's presence in the world. The Bible says that God is a historical reality, who heals man's sins. That this is a matter of faith makes human existence a struggle for something obtainable only at the cost of great exertion. Moreover sin strives to banish from human life this God who is a historical reality healing man's sinfulness. Scriptural asceticism is based on recognition of these facts and derives its essential meaning only from them.

If we describe Christian life as an ascent toward perfect union with God, we can see asceticism as man's uninterrupted endeavor in this earthly life to open himself to the fullness of God's healing love — which fullness is embodied in Christ (cf. Col. 2:9). The fact that this reality can be known only through faith and that we are sinners can make it necessary — sometimes even because of a special vocation from God — to exemplify this ascetic attitude by ascetic practices.

REFERENCES

1. Cf. R. Schnackenburg's article "Askese," in: *Lexikon für Theologie und Kirche* I, 930-932.

2. Here we have let ourselves be inspired by K. Rahner in his *Nieuwe Thelogische Verkenningstochten*, Haarlem 1961, pp. 61-71. However we have modified his definitions a little.

3. Cf. R. Bultmann *Nederl. Kath. Stemmen* 1961: the essays of J. B. W. Moller, pp. 233-243 and of J. Kahmann, pp. 244-254.

4. Cf. in the monthly *Het heilig Land* 1960 the essays of H. Verhaeghe, pp. 70-71; 84-85; F. Lenssen, *The Bible about the Exodus* (Roermond 1964).

5. Cf. Jos. Schmid, article "Reinheit," in *Lexikon für Theologie und Kirche*, 8., 1145-1148 and P. van Imschoot, article "Rein," in *Bijbels Woordenboek,* 2nd ed. 1456-1458.

6. Cf. J. Chaine, *Le Livre de la Genèse*, Paris 1948, pp. 268; 274.

7. Cf. G. Ernest Wright, *De Bijbel ontdekt in aarde en steen,* Baarn 1958, pp. 82-83.

8. Cf. G. Ernest Wright, o.c. (note 7) p. 134.

9. Cf. J. Steinmann, *St. Jean-Baptiste et la spiritualité du désert,* Paris 1955.

10. Cf. A. Néher, *L'Essence du Prophétisme, Paris 1955*, pp. 166-175.

11. Cf. C. J. De Vogel, "Het probleem van het kwade in de Antieke Wijsbegeerte," in: *Studia Catholica* 27 (1952), pp. 20-38.

12. Cf. J. T. Nelis, in: *Bijbels Woordenboek,* 2nd ed., article "Dodenrijk" 355-356 and "Sheol," 1576-1577.

13. Cf. P. Schoonenberg, in *Tijdschrift voor Theologie* 1 (1961), p. 196.

14. Cf. A. Hulsbosch, "De eschatologie van het Boek der Wijsheid," in *Stud. Cath.* 27 (1952), pp. 113-123.

15. Cf. E. Schillebeeckx," De dood van een Christen," in: *Kultuurleven* 22 (1955), pp. 421-430 and 508-519.